# Religion & Spirituality in the Public School Curriculum

PETER LANG
New York • Washington, D.C./Baltimore • Bern
Frankfurt am Main • Berlin • Brussels • Vienna • Oxford

Ronald D. Anderson

# Religion & Spirituality in the Public School Curriculum

PETER LANG
New York • Washington, D.C./Baltimore • Bern
Frankfurt am Main • Berlin • Brussels • Vienna • Oxford

**Library of Congress Cataloging-in-Publication Data**

Anderson, Ronald D.
Religion and spirituality in the public school curriculum /
Ronald D. Anderson.
p. cm.
Includes bibliographical references and index.
1. Religion in the public schools—United States. 2. Public
schools—United States—Curricula. 3. Teaching—Religious aspects.
4. Education—Philosophy. 5. Spiritual life. I. Title.
LC111.A89    379.2'8'0973—dc21    2003003751
ISBN 0-8204-5807-4


Bibliographic information published by **Die Deutsche Bibliothek**.
**Die Deutsche Bibliothek** lists this publication in the "Deutsche
Nationalbibliografie"; detailed bibliographic data is available
on the Internet at http://dnb.ddb.de/.

Cover design by Lisa Barfield
Cover photo by David K. Wendt


The paper in this book meets the guidelines for permanence and durability
of the Committee on Production Guidelines for Book Longevity
of the Council of Library Resources.

© 2004 Peter Lang Publishing, Inc., New York
275 Seventh Avenue, 28th Floor, New York, NY 10001
www.peterlangusa.com

Printed in the United States of America

# TABLE OF CONTENTS

# ACKNOWLEDGMENTS

Giving proper credit to all the people who have in some way influenced this book is an impossible task. At least indirectly, the book has been developing over a period of many years, and there is no way to identify all who have shaped my thinking on the topic. One hint of these influences, of course, is the bibliography at the end of the book. Even among those authors with whom I have fundamental disagreements are ones who have shaped my thinking. Miscellaneous conversations with colleagues, class discussions with students, and conference forums have all made important contributions.

Of more direct importance are a number of people who read an initial draft of the manuscript and gave me their reactions. They included Tara Barneson, Bill Cobern, David Jackson, Patricia Jessup, Richard Kraft, Daniel Liston, Beverly Parsons, and John Staver. All of their suggestions did not find their way into the manuscript but nevertheless, their thoughtful comments were both helpful and greatly appreciated.

Although they entered the process of developing this book near its conclusion, Judith Nowlin and Lisa Loranger made a big contribution to its production. Their secretarial, computer, and publishing expertise made the transition from initial manuscript to final book a process that demanded very little from me. Peter Lang Publishing has been a great firm to work with, and of the many people there who had a part in producing this book, thanks particularly must be directed to Phyllis Korper, Jackie Pavlovic, and Sophie Appel.

Appreciation is expressed to Charles Haynes and the First Amendment Center for permission to reprint as an appendix to this book their statement titled *A Teacher's Guide to Religion in the Public Schools*. It is an excellent description of the political, legal, and societal context so important to this book.

A big debt of gratitude is owed to the John Templeton Foundation for a grant that enabled me to devote more professional time to this endeavor in its early stages than would otherwise have been possible. Paul Wasson and others at the Foundation have been both supportive and encouraging.

Finally, and most importantly, my thanks to my wife, Sandy, for assistance and support in so many tangible and intangible ways. Among the obvious tangible contributions is her computer expertise, which extends beyond that available in reference manuals and help lines. But, of course, that contribution pales alongside of all her other contributions to my life.

# ONE

## *Introduction*

Amerian society is a blend of secularized and religious elements that poses a dilemma for public education—how to accommodate both societal characteristics. The dilemma is as present today as it has ever been, and it clamors for attention. Some degree of resolution of the dilemma is not only desirable but possible.

Secularization is one of the major themes of modern history. It has roots in the scientific and technological nature of our society, but also in our pluralism. In the Western world today, political discussions and public social discourse can proceed with little reference to God or attention to individual persons' understandings of relating to God. Because our society is highly pluralistic, there is no common understanding of the underlying order. As a result of our pluralism we naturally gravitate to matters of common understanding in public discourse, and this discourse then is conducted in secular terms.

Spirituality and religion have not disappeared from the modern or postmodern world, although they may be displayed in quite different ways from in the past. Opinion polls show very high levels of belief in God. The percentage of people who participate weekly in religious services in the United States is substantial (in contrast to Europe). But the pluralistic nature of these beliefs (including nonbelief) means that the social compact is expressed in other terms. As modernity has evolved, it increasingly has focused on the benefits for individuals and the protection of individual rights, with a correspondingly lesser focus on matters of community—including religious community.

It is important for students to understand this aspect of history and the secular character of our political and social life. It should be one of the themes of modern history as taught in the schools. At the same time, the picture of our society and culture presented to students should be accurate in the sense of not leaving out the fact that religion and spirituality are important within the contemporary setting as well; they are not just relics of the past. The United States is both plural and religious.

## The Context of Our Dilemma

The secular nature of American public culture and its underlying pluralistic character are important aspects of the context for our system of education. In any historical review—or contemporary global comparison—the United States stands out both in terms of the degree of pluralism and in having a political system that seems to accommodate it. A central question for us is how public education in this context can accommodate this pluralism and provide an education that is complete and authentic—for example, does not ignore or marginalize religious or spiritual elements—for the full sweep of this plural student population.

Pluralism is an increasingly prominent aspect of our society. This diversity in both racial and religious identity continues to grow. While at one time it would have been quite accurate to describe the religious makeup of the United States as Protestant, Catholic, and Jewish, the situation is more diverse today. Some keepers of statistics say the United States now has more Muslims than Jews, and the presence of various Eastern and Native American religions is notable as well, even though the total percentage of Christians of all stripes combined within the population has remained fairly constant. The diversity of religious beliefs—and nonbelief—gives every indication of growing. It is a social reality which is reflected in the school population and which the schools must address.

Multiculturalism as an educational movement has given important and significant attention to this pluralism and diversity in terms of gender, ethnic, and racial matters. Our diversity with respect to religion and spirituality has not received comparable attention, though many would claim it deserves it. The goal of this book is to address how spirituality and religion can be given their due in this context.

## Schools Reflect Secular and Religious Aspects of Society

Schools are a reflection of their society. What is playing out in the schools reflects issues in the society at large. What is taught and how it is taught are an outgrowth of the secular character of our modern society. As noted earlier, this secular character does not mean an absence of God and religion. God can be very present for many people, but this presence is not assumed for everyone, and thus our common discourse is not based on a universal assumption of God as an influential agent. Of course, not everyone has the same interpretation of this situation. Philosopher Charles Taylor describes an alternative understanding:

...moving to a society where more and more the consensus will be around an unbelieving variant of the modern social imaginary. But to me this seems to be just a dream. It's a dream that arises among those who are deeply into an atheist or non-believing position and are convinced as a matter of faith that religion will gradually disappear and everyone will think as they do. For them, the secular world is one in which we all end up agreeing fundamentally that there's no God, and that agreement is the basis of everything. That's an impossible scenario.... (Benson, 2002)

Like Taylor, I am prepared to approach social issues with the expectation that the religious character of our society will persist—although probably in a constantly changing form.

## Politics Are Part of the Context

Public education is fully embedded in a political context. At the national level, it can be seen in the deliberations of the Congress, the actions of the Executive branch of government, and the positions of professional organizations. The Congress chooses among competing interest groups in its consideration of legislation supporting such specific areas as bilingual education, special education, and science education, as well as legislation that supports a particular orientation to education in general. The Executive branch attempts to influence such Congressional decisions and takes particular approaches to implementing legislation. National political action is also illustrated by the work of national professional organizations, with the development of content standards for various subject areas serving as a good example. Typically, standards in such fields as mathematics, history, and science were developed by their respective professional associations, such as the National Council of Teachers of Mathematics, with input from not only teachers but essentially all relevant organizations, such as the various professional associations of mathematicians. Federal grant money may have partially supported the work, but it was done by professional associations. National political influences are part of the context of public education.

*Other levels.* Since only about 7 percent of the funding for public education comes from the Federal government—with the remainder coming from state and local monies—it is not surprising that the main political actions are at these same state and local levels. State governments—all three branches—are involved in shaping teacher education programs, state programs of testing student achievement, programs for students with special needs, and potential or actual charter school programs or voucher programs, and making decisions about the equalization of funding across poor and rich school districts.

Although the educational balance of power between state and local government varies substantially among the states, the local political context of schooling is always very important. The citizens of a local school district often become deeply engaged in debates over such matters as middle schools versus alternative structures of schooling for this age group, the role and influence of athletic programs, the relative emphasis on art and music programs versus "hard-core" academics, and even required uniforms for elementary school students and public prayer at football games.

**Value questions.** At the root of all these political deliberations and power struggles are a host of value questions. To what extent should, or can, public education accommodate individual differences with respect to academic ability, cultural background, worldviews, various disabilities, etc.? What is the appropriate balance between the arts and the three Rs? What place should religion and spirituality have? Such specific questions—and the even more specific questions pertaining to a particular school or classroom—are grounded in broader, more philosophical questions. What is the purpose of education? What is the nature of learning—and of teaching? The lists go on.

**Economic considerations.** Yet another aspect of this political context that must be recognized is the need to educate masses of students with financial resources that apparently preclude educating each student individually. Public education follows a pattern sometimes referred to as a "factory model." Mass education using currently appropriated resources that also is individualized and provides for the full range of individual differences is generally perceived by policymakers to be unrealistic. So, another aspect of the political context is that we have mass education that has only limited aspects of individualization.

Within this overall political context, many decisions are made that are not optimum for all students. In some cases, a choice is made between two sharply differing positions, with the result that one side loses and another wins, and thus some students win and others lose. In other cases a compromise is reached that is more or less acceptable to all sides, but all students' needs are not met. Although many such decisions are intended to accommodate all students within the system—and diversity and all cultures are said to be valued—there is no way to avoid the fact that these political decisions result in an education that rarely is ideal for most individuals. Public education potentially yields the "common school" with all its benefits for a democratic society, but it must also be granted that it is difficult to provide mass education (public or private) that truly meets the needs of all.

## Controversies Abound

As a result of value questions and economic considerations, the schools are the focal point of many public controversies today. The reform of education is a hot political issue, a matter to which we will return in a later chapter. The partisans on the various sides of these issues often cross party lines. In addition to the general concern about the improvement of education, there are a number of specific issues, many of which—though not all—have religious roots. Some issues have been with us in a somewhat consistent form for nearly a century, such as the controversy over the teaching of evolution. As in the case of the controversy over school prayer, the court decisions on the issue are quite clear-cut, but political maneuvering persists. But court decisions by themselves often are an inadequate basis for full resolution of an issue, as we shall see when we examine some of these specific issues. The landmark court decisions typically are a necessary, but not sufficient, basis for resolving an issue.

Among the current prominent issues at this writing are the place of vouchers and charter schools. Vouchers provide public money that parents can use at a private school of their choice. They are politically popular in many circles because they give parents a choice among schools and seemingly are a way that parents can find the best schooling for their children. They also are the source of much debate for a complex set of reasons. Although a full examination of this debate is not the focus of this book, it is important to note that there is a religious dimension to the debate in that a majority of the private schools at which such vouchers are used are religious schools. Another focus of debate is charter schools, which are alternative public schools that generally operate outside the direct supervisory mechanisms of local school districts. Religion usually is not central to this controversy, although some parents seek a particular charter school for personal reasons which have a religious basis.

### Our Focus—Curriculum and Teaching

A number of sources of tension in the public schools regarding religion have been mentioned here, but all are not central to this book. Our focus is limited to public schools and within that context is limited to matters of curriculum and approaches to teaching. It has to do with what goes on in classrooms and not such matters as prayer at all school events or student religious clubs in the schools—for a widely accepted consensus statement on these latter matters, see the appendix. To what extent should information about religion and its influences be part of the curriculum in a subject such as history? To what extent should students be allowed—or encouraged—to express themselves in the classroom concerning who they are as persons in a religious or spiritual sense? To what extent should the alternative worldviews of individual students—

coming from varied religious perspectives—be heard? Should any worldviews be given favored status? Questions of this nature are our focus, along with consideration of how answers to such questions play out in practice in classrooms.

While this entire book will be utilized in developing answers to these questions, I will present some of the underlying arguments in summary form at this point. In addition, I will indicate how the various components of this story will be distributed over the subsequent chapters.

## A Complete Education

We need to take into account the nature of schooling as it exists in our society. We must recognize that public education—or private schooling for that matter—rarely is complete in scope and coverage. In addition to the traditional academic disciplines and the arts, a truly complete education also must address personal matters—which, of course, vary from student to student. These include aspects of life such as religion and spirituality, which American public education tends to avoid for a number of reasons, including a perceived need for "separation of church and state." The provision of a complete education is constrained by the political context of public education, including the limitations of mass schooling.

But just what is an authentic and complete education? Answering this question is not quick and easy. In fact, a substantial section of this book will be devoted to this question, beginning with careful consideration of the purposes of education and the nature of learning and teaching. Prior to dealing with details, however, we can identify some key points. First, an authentic and complete education demands attention to a broad sweep of areas of human understanding and experience. While basic and important, the three Rs do not constitute a complete education, even at the beginning levels. Such subjects as art and music have an important place in education. And within basic areas, the mechanics of reading and writing, for example, are not adequate by themselves. This is not to diminish their importance, but by themselves they are not enough. A student must be able to use basic skills to express a broad range of concepts and emotions and be able to understand them in the writing of others. Similarly, within a specific area care must be taken to include the full sweep of perspectives. A well-documented example of a lack of such coverage in American public schooling is the failure to give adequate treatment to the role of religion in world history (Nord, 1995).

Secondly, fully representative coverage is not enough; students must be assisted with making interconnections among the parts of this broad coverage. The research is clear; without assistance, students see relatively few of the connections and generally do not transfer their understandings from one realm to another. For example, while an understanding of fundamental concepts in a field such as science is central, one's science education is not complete without some attention to the implications of this understanding for individual matters such as health and nutrition or for societal issues involving economic and environmental considerations. Similarly, even though enjoyment of a piece of music does not necessarily require a knowledge of its origins, a full understanding of this music is not possible without an understanding of the social, cultural, and historical context from which it came.

Thirdly, an authentic education must in important senses be personal. Whether it is a matter of one's personal experience of music, the application of aspects of biology to one's particular personal health issues, or the personal insights gained from a piece of literature, there is an important personal dimension. This attention to the personal dimension, of course, does *not* mean that students should be indoctrinated in some particular personal interpretation of a piece of music or literature. The fear that children will be pressured into certain personal understandings is at the root of some parents' desire for the curriculum to be as narrow as possible. They want to avoid any possibility that their children will be asked to "believe" anything contrary to the child's or family's convictions. The result is a dilemma for some parents: How can my child's education be complete and authentic without someone telling my child what to believe in areas where various people have differing perspectives? It is the thesis of this book that, given the right approach, the dilemma is more perceived than real.

## Religion and Spirituality Must Get Their Due

Providing an authentic and complete education is of great importance. Without attention to complete coverage, helping students make interconnections, and drawing attention to the many personal dimensions of a topic, the education students receive is not only limited and truncated; it ends up being distorted and the source of misconceptions. For example, if the many religious influences on world history are omitted from the curriculum, or de-emphasized, students probably will not understand religion's relative influence on history and its importance in many people's lives. If students do not understand the differences in the "ways of knowing" in science and various religious traditions, they will not fully understand the ongoing creation versus evolution battle, which is experienced very differently by students from different faith traditions. Because students experience this battle—and other aspects of what is often called the culture wars—in such a personal way, their education is far from complete unless they bring into the picture their personal perspectives.

Survey data show that matters of religion and spirituality are important aspects of life for the great majority of people in the United States, including the students in our schools. And even for students who do not claim any allegiance to a religious perspective, their secular perspective is an answer to questions all people face concerning the nature of reality, the purpose (or purposelessness) of life, and what gives them meaning (Noddings, 1993). In other words, a student's worldview is highly relevant to his or her education. Unless education goes deep enough to bring such matters to the fore, it has failed.

The fact that public education generally does fail in this sense may be an indication of the challenges in making education what it should be. The failure to adequately address these matters generally is not due to real constitutional or legislative constraints; it generally is due to a number of other factors, including misconceptions about legal constraints, narrow conceptions of the nature of education, and what Stephen Carter (1993) has called the general "culture of disbelief." The challenges are many and not easy to overcome. There is a tension resulting from the complex political context in which public education exists on the one hand, and on the other the very nature of an authentic and complete education. In many ways the context of public schooling and the demands of a complete and authentic education are incompatible with each other. This tension and potential means of reducing it are central to this book.

## Addressing the Dilemma

The dilemma is obvious. Due to its political context—including the financial constraints which yield mass schooling—public education tends to be impersonal and leave out facets of life essential to a "complete education." Yet, a complete education is of critical importance. Can the constraints on public education be overcome and significant progress made toward providing this essential complete education? The thesis of this book is that significant progress in resolving this dilemma is possible and the means of making this progress are available. While this dilemma will not be totally resolved, significant progress in many areas is possible, including some of the areas thought to be among the more difficult, namely religion and spirituality.

Many parents in this country have in essence said that the dilemma has no immediate resolution and have resorted to private schools, home schooling, and charter schools. While I am supportive of parents who make these choices, I am not ready to give up on the public schools. In fact, I am persuaded that the presence of a strong and vital public education system is essential for the future of our democratic society. Options for parents are important—including private schools, home schooling, and charter schools—but the most important option is a strong public school system which provides for individual differences among students—including differences with respect to worldview, religion, spirituality—*and* which encourages reflection upon alternative perspectives and growth in understanding. In particular, the focus of this book is to address those aspects of a complete education that are in some manner connected to religion and spirituality.

## Centrality of Worldviews

Specifics of how this complete education can be attained will be addressed within different curricular areas in later chapters, but one generalization deserves specific mention here, namely no particular worldview should dominate or receive undue attention. Such imbalance can occur either consciously or unconsciously, either overtly or covertly. Two examples appear in the contemporary "culture wars" of the public square. Some portions—though certainly not all—of the so-called Christian Right seem irrevocably attached to the idea that prayer and Bible reading of a devotional sort should be in the school program, along with religiously based character education. Clearly, these notions are out of step with our particular democratic form of government and our Constitution as interpreted by the courts. Given our pluralistic society, such approaches are untenable and would lead to great conflict. This slant toward a particular worldview is out of the question.

A second example of an unacceptable approach is one often attributed to the "cultural elite," or more specifically, the "academic elite." In some ways analogous to the pressure just mentioned from the right, it is a view that insists that religion and spirituality be privatized and kept from the public square. In its more extreme form, it seeks schooling based on a worldview that assumes no God, no spiritual reality, and no overarching purpose to history or to life beyond that which a particular individual chooses. Again, it is a worldview that is untenable as an operating basis for the schools because it is not inclusive. Neither of these two extremes is at all acceptable. We are left with working out a more centrist position that is based on democratic principles, honors the individual and is equitable for all within our diverse populace. This position cannot be derived from some idea of a "least common denominator," but must be a robust approach that provides for individual students who may identify themselves with either of these polar opposites.

## Our Purposes and Goals

While the entirety of this book will be used to develop this view of what education should be, its core can be summarized very briefly here. Education is more than transmitting knowledge to students; it is a process of active engagement by individual students that requires teacher facilitation. It is individual education, not simply mass education. Authentic education is not impersonal; it is a unique process for each individual, a process in which the individual's engagement with the subject matter is personal and connects with their basic values, beliefs, and worldview. Ideally, this individual process occurs in the context of an educational community where very different individuals have some mutuality of experiences that result in quite varied outcomes. Chapters 2 and 3 will be devoted to elaborating this position. Chapter 4 will be a bit of a detour for those who may need the background before going on to addressing the nature of the curriculum.

## The Nature of the Curriculum

Many people see little hope of resolving this dilemma in the context of United States public schooling. In their view, schooling is public and religion is private; thus education cannot really be complete. But much depends upon how one conceives of schooling and the nature of the curriculum. Within the American context, many different characterizations of the curriculum have been advanced and debated—characterizations that vary greatly in terms of educational goals, the actions of teachers, the experiences of students, and learning outcomes. The overall task before us—resolving the dilemma—requires that we consider in-depth alternative understandings of the curriculum and how they would play out in practice with respect to the issues at hand. To what extent do we conceive of the curriculum as subject matter to be taught, as a program of planned activities, as learning outcomes to be tested, as experiences students should have, or as self-understandings that should be sought? Early on, we will need to grapple with these alternatives and consider how they relate to providing students with a complete education. The posture I will take is that there is a conception of the curriculum that can be the basis for resolving our dilemma. Chapter 5 will be devoted to describing this characterization of the curriculum and how it can serve our purposes.

## Those Ever-Present Worldviews

The previously mentioned matter of students' worldviews is central to the approach I am advocating. Students have varied understandings of what purpose their life has, what constitutes reality, and whether or not there is a God. Their understandings extend to matters of moral choice, their conception of character, and their understandings of themselves. Such matters are central to one's education, and given an orientation to the curriculum such as I am advocating here, it is possible for this aspect of education to become an important aspect of formal schooling as well. Chapter 6 is devoted to this matter of students' worldviews and personal spirituality.

## Case Studies

While my general argument is made in the first six chapters, I need to make the portrayal specific and tangible. I present four case studies in chapters 7 through 10 for that purpose. The first is the most specific in that it deals with one small facet of a subject area, namely the teaching of evolution within the science curriculum. The next two are much broader and address entire subject areas, namely literature and history. Finally, in chapter 10 I turn to the imposing topic of character or values education. The case studies give us an opportunity to see what the general principles look like in practice, as well as how feasible they may be in the real world.

## Making It Happen

Even if one is convinced that the ideas presented here in broad outline—and in specific case studies—are desirable, feasible, and worthy of initiating in school practice, there is still the question of how they can be put into actual practice. For one teacher to put these ideas into practice in an actual school setting—even on a wildly successful basis—would provide little assurance that they could be implemented on a mass basis. Such change is not easy—in fact, it is extremely difficult. The next three chapters tackle the process of making such change on an extended basis. The approach I am advocating gives major roles to families and faith communities; this topic is the center of chapter 11.

Educational reform is a prominent matter in the schools of today. Many approaches to reform are being pursued—some worthwhile and others inconsequential or even harmful. These approaches also have been the subject of many useful research studies. In chapter 12 I apply some of these principles to the question of how school practice realistically could be changed to give religion and spirituality their due.

One aspect of any viable effort for pursuing educational change is teacher education. Whether it is part of a program for the initial certification of new teachers or a program of education for teachers on the job, systematic teacher education efforts are almost certainly an important part of the picture. Chapter 13 tackles the question of what can be done in this arena to further the cause of moving religion and spirituality into their appropriate place in public education.

### Audience for This Book

The audience I am addressing in this book is primarily people who have a direct influence over what takes place in public schools, including teachers, administrators, policymakers (such as school board members), and people involved in educating teachers. This latter group, teacher educators, overlaps partially with the academic community, many of whom tend to have one foot in the practical world of schooling and the other in the academy. This book is about what goes on in schools, but it is addressed from an academic perspective.

While I am a member of the academic community and I hope that many of my academic colleagues will read this book, I have not written it primarily for them. If such were the case, I would expect to go deeper in each of the several sections of the book in terms of documentation and elaboration of various facets of the argument. Thus, in some senses this book provides an overview of an argument that could be pursued in considerably greater detail.

The argument I am making is based on understandings drawn from many different academic areas. It is built upon the nature of learning, conceptions of teaching, alternative views of the curriculum, the nature of various academic subjects, the nature of religion, the varieties of spiritual experiences, the legal foundations for both education and religion in this country, the nature of our culture and many subcultures, and more. Each of these facets could be explored in much more detail than I have done here, but my main focus is the overall argument and I have delved into each of these areas with the level of detail I think appropriate for making my argument within a book of this length.

## Personal Perspectives

It must be acknowledged that a certain amount of idealism permeates this book. I do not want to settle for the status quo; our public education has the potential for being much better than it is—not just in terms of higher achievement within schools as they are currently conceptualized and operated, but in a reformed version that attends to a more complete education, with a broader sweep of goals including aspects of what goes under the labels of spiritual and religious. Some may say that the realities of our economic, social, cultural, and legal context are such that this acknowledged idealism is wasted effort or "tilting at windmills." But idealism can also be a source of vision, and a vision of what could be is of vital importance if one wants positive change. Furthermore, realism and the practical are not ignored, as will be found in the later chapters on family and community involvement, educational reform, and teacher education. With a vision for what could be, we have a chance to make changes in the "real world."

### Personal Convictions

It is fair to expect that the author of a book on a topic such as religion and education would identify the perspective from which he is operating. To begin with, I am committed to a democratic society and public education. Although I am persuaded that a democratic society is strengthened by—and probably requires—parental choice between public and private education for their children, I am deeply committed to a strong public school system. It is important for the maintenance of our democratic way of life, especially given the plural nature of our society.

I am also a person with religious convictions. Identifying them for the reader is a bit more difficult, however, given the inadequacy of some labels and the various ways they are used. My initial inclination is simply to identify myself as a Christian, but some people associate this term with the religious right or institutional forms of religion, associations that are not really apt. An appropriate way of expressing it would be to say that I consider myself an apprentice of Jesus of Nazareth. My Christian convictions are of a quite orthodox sort. Being part of a community of other apprentices is an important part of this picture, but it is not a matter of being a member of a religious system or institution. The relationship with the divine is understood as personal and it influences the nature of this community. All of this is not about some loosely held opinions, but about in-depth convictions that shape who I am as a person and how I live my life.

These brief comments may elicit a desire for elaboration about my understanding of words such as *tolerance* and *community*. An expression of strong and specific convictions, such as the above, raises concerns among some that the holder of such convictions does not understand what it means to be tolerant of others. On the contrary, it may be that someone who holds firm and specific convictions may have a greater understanding of tolerance as a result of recognizing that convictions of this nature vary greatly within our pluralistic society and that many of these convictions are deeply held. To recognize this reality and to also have a deep respect and, yes, even love, for all of humanity is a source of tolerance. In contrast, it is possible for the dogmatic relativist to be quite intolerant if this person's outlook on humanity does not include a high regard for all people, including those with convictions other than relativistic ones.

I am also convinced of the importance of community. Our pluralistic society and the depth of the varied convictions within it lead to multiple understandings of community. As a democratic society it is important that we have a significant sense of community that encompasses the entire populace. This need for community extends to the school as well; a sense of school community is important. Both within society as a whole and within a particular school, however, individuals will have other experiences of community, some of which may be personally more important to the particular individual than the general community. Various religious communities, or subgroups within them, may constitute particularly important communities for some students. These multiple and overlapping communities are of vital importance to students and must be recognized in the way we operate schools. Schooling must be conducted in a manner that takes into account students' affiliation with these varied communities. To not take it into account is to diminish—and to some extent trivialize—their education.

Although I have put the Christian label on myself, my intent has *not* been to write this book from a Christian perspective. It is written from a religious perspective, however, in that religious belief and experience has been accepted as valid and real, with no thought that it should be explained away in secular or naturalistic terms. At the same time there is the desire to fully accept as friend or colleague others around me who do explain it away in such a manner. The presumption is that the commitment I share with so many others to honoring our diversity and building a civil and democratic society demands that varied commitments to religion or non-religion, belief or nonbelief, piety or non-piety, be fully accepted, honored, and supported in our civil discourse and life together.

# TWO

# *The Nature of a Complete Education*

## Purposes and Emphases

What constitutes a good education? Our answer to this question has profound implications; it shapes any discussion we have about schooling. The question has been posed in quite varied ways. One famous framing of the issue was to ask, "What knowledge is of most worth?" While I find this question very important, I prefer not to set it forth as the sole or even primary question because it presupposes an answer to the one I started with, "What constitutes a good education?" A good education includes more than particular knowledge. If I were to depart from my original framing of the issue, I would be tempted to ask what constitutes a *complete* education, since a good education has so many facets. But even identifying all the facets is not enough to describe a good education, since so much depends upon how each facet is handled by the teacher, and holistically how the educational process is handled as well, since the sum of the parts does not constitute the whole.

Once we have developed the ideas underlying a complete education, we can turn our attention to the place of spirituality and religion in such an education. That will be our topic in the chapter following this one.

To seek a "complete" education is no small undertaking, since the purposes of education are so many and varied, resulting in such complexities and lengthiness that the task may seem overwhelming. The norm for U.S. education is to have multiple purposes, resulting in competition for space in the curriculum and public debates about schooling.

The multiplicity of purposes is evident in the educational literature. A fairly recent listing of such purposes by Goodlad (1994) included the following:

mastery of basic skills or fundamental processes
career education
interpersonal relations
autonomy

citizenship
creativity
self-realization
intellectual development
enculturation
self-concept
emotional and physical well-being
moral and ethical character

Many, possibly most, debates about education are debates about relative emphasis among these many purposes. Although we can never "do it all," we are faced with the challenges of doing as much as possible—with the necessary focus and appropriate pedagogy—such that the results are deserving of the label, a "complete education."

The debates over educational purposes take many forms. A prevalent form is a debate between "basic skills" and a more conceptual approach that emphasizes conceptual understanding of knowledge, its origins and its applications. As we entered the twenty-first century, one highly visible version of these debates was the tug-of-war over a basic skills approach to teaching mathematics and a more conceptual or process-oriented approach. In specific form, the debate often came down to a battle over "Saxon math" versus textbooks that followed the guidelines of the National Council of Teachers of Mathematics (1989). In another arena the debate was between a phonics and a "whole language" approach to teaching reading in elementary schools. A sad aspect of these debates is their highly polarized character and lack of sound reference to research data. The debate as portrayed by newspaper columnists, postings on the Internet, or hearings in front of school boards tended to posit a choice between the forces of good and evil. One had to decide which side was the good guys and which was the bad guys. Ideally, the debate would not be so polarized and would be a dialogue about matters of emphasis. People seeking a balanced approach with an openness to the results of research and arguments from alternative perspectives are needed in these battles. Given the nature of our culture, however, dialogue is unlikely to replace debate any time soon.

Debates about relative emphases among our host of educational purposes take other forms as well. Some individuals, for example, distinguish between academic growth and goals such as developing autonomy, self-realization, self-concept, and emotional and physical well-being. While essentially everyone is a proponent of academic growth, some would largely limit the curriculum to it and curtail work on goals, such as the above, related to personal growth. On the other hand are people convinced that fully successful attainment of the academic goals requires attention to matters of personal growth and, furthermore, that these goals are important in their own right.

It would be easy to launch into a more detailed discussion of these issues at this point and stake out a position on them. To do so, however, runs the risk of perpetuating the acrimonious debates that characterize so much of public discourse on these topics. A more detailed and nuanced discussion is needed. We need a close look at such matters as the nature of learning, alternative understandings of teaching, the nature of human intelligence(s), and alternative worldviews found within our culture. With that grounding it will be possible to turn to discussing the purposes of education in a manner that generates more light and less heat.

## Multiple Intelligences

The advent of paper-and-pencil intelligence tests early in the last century may have reinforced the proclivity of schools to focus on linguistic and mathematical tasks with reduced dedication to the arenas of beauty and virtue:

> Intelligence tests typically tap linguistic and logical-mathematical intelligence—the intelligences of greatest moment in contemporary schools—perhaps sampling spatial intelligence as well. (Gardner, 1999, p. 72)

As the current century began, music and fine arts were in decline in most schools and physical education for the average student was eclipsed by competitive sports for the athletically gifted with their concomitant entertainment and celebrity aspirations. It was as if the life of the mind was very narrowly defined and a good education had relatively few major components. There are a lot of reasons for this limited conception of education, but they probably are not unrelated to our narrow understanding of what constitutes human intelligence—an understanding that has begun to break down as psychologists have continued to pursue the questions of what constitutes human intelligence and how it can be measured.

Psychologist Howard Gardner has been influential in bringing to public awareness a broader understanding of intelligence. In addition to the previously mentioned linguistic, logical-mathematical, and spatial intelligences, he posits five or six additional dimensions of human intelligence:

> But as a species we also possess musical intelligence, bodily-kinesthetic intelligence, naturalistic intelligence, intelligence about ourselves (intrapersonal intelligence), and intelligence about other persons (interpersonal intelligence). And it is possible that human beings also exhibit a ninth, existential intelligence—the proclivity to pose (and ponder) questions about life, death, and ultimate realities. Each of these intelligences

features its own distinctive form of mental representation; in fact, it is equally accurate to say that each intelligence *is* a form of mental representation. (Gardner, 2000, p. 72)

While we will be unable to examine this topic in much greater depth, it is important that we explore the educational implications of this broader understanding of intelligence. It is of central importance for our discussion of education. It lends support to the notion of a complete education as defined here. This complete education is more than the "three Rs" and gives attention to—among others—music, the arts, interpersonal relationships, and the spiritual. To focus on the former intelligences to the restriction of these additional ones is to narrowly circumscribe the life of the mind and also encourage a limited understanding of those intelligences that do find a place in the curriculum.

Gardner also notes that not only are there multiple intelligences, but there are large individual differences in the degrees to which they are present in people. The proportions in which they are exhibited varies, and they are displayed in quite different patterns across individuals, with substantial educational implications:

This fact poses intriguing challenges and opportunities for our educational system. We can ignore these differences and pretend that we are all the same; historically, that is what most educational systems have done. Or we can fashion an educational system that tries to exploit these differences, individualizing instruction and assessment as much as possible. (Gardner, 1999, p. 71)

Our desired education is broad, deep, and rich. Theoretical aspects of science are important in their own right, but their application to personal and societal issues is critical as well. Classical literature has direct value, but in addition, students should come to appreciate how literary expression relates to their personal circumstances and enriches their engagement with life and its many issues. An understanding of the contributions of the musical classics can be an important component of one's education, but personal musical expression can play a major role in the life of students as well.

At first blush, what is portrayed here is a matter of the content of the curriculum. But it is more—much more. How one engages with this content is of equal importance. What does it mean to learn something? Is it simply transmitting understandings to the minds of students, or does it require a certain form of engagement with the content on the part of students? And what does it mean to *engage* this content?

## The Nature of Learning

A student in one of my graduate courses for teachers employed in the "real world" returned from her library search for resources with a mixture of excitement and reticence—sort of a good news–bad news story. She had set off on her search because her study had convinced her she was obligated (legally, ethically, and intellectually) to give her students a more complete picture of the influence of religion on historical events than was found in the curriculum materials of her school. In the process she examined the "Core Knowledge" materials of E. D. Hirsch (1987). Her enthusiasm was the result of finding some materials that had more of the desired content than she had found thus far in any other curriculum materials she had examined. Within these materials she found the curriculum content for which she had been searching. Her restraint, on the other hand, was due to another characteristic of the program. In her view, the teaching approaches in which the content was embedded were based on an understanding of the nature of learning that was problematic. She recognized that how students learn and how one teaches are quite different matters from the content of the curriculum itself. She had found some of the content she was seeking, but it was rooted within a pedagogical system she did not want to adopt. Since she is a teacher with a high level of professional competence, however, she made good use of what she found. She was able to take from the materials the content she was seeking—without adopting the total content package she may or may not have judged appropriate—and put it into her own teaching approach, grounded in her personal understanding of the nature of learning.

What are these different understandings of the nature of learning that are of such major significance to a teacher—and anyone else making educational decisions? At the risk of oversimplifying, these different understandings will be presented here as a dichotomy—two alternative understandings of learning. The one I will identify by a fairly common label within the educational world—the *transmission* understanding or model of learning. The alternative understanding of learning I will call the *constructivist* model.

Labels are often problematic and *constructivist* is a prime example of such. At this point, I am using the word as a label for an understanding of how people learn. To avoid confusion, some people who talk about constructivism in this sense expand the label and refer to *psychological constructivism* or *cognitive constructivism*. On the other hand, some persons use the label, *constructivism*, in a different sense, a sense which they may clarify by expanding the label to *social constructivism*. In this sense, *constructivism* (or less commonly *constructionist*) is largely an epistemological matter of what constitutes "truth"; it has been part of the "culture wars" of our day. (To make matters worse, some writers have adopted the label *social constructivism* to describe an approach to teaching that depends upon a considerable amount of interaction among students. But this use of the term is far less common and I will not use it in this manner in this book.) To clarify the situation here, let me note that when I use the term in this book—unless clearly indicated otherwise—I am referring to *cognitive constructivism*, an understanding of how a person learns or mentally acquires new understandings. The two versions of constructivism, *cognitive* and *social*, are quite different matters, although some writers see them as closely related. A person kindly disposed to one is not necessarily enamored with the other. For the moment, you are being asked to recognize that they are quite different from each other. And if your understanding of constructivism is derived from discussions about social constructivism, you are being asked to attempt to set it aside while we explore cognitive constructivism as an understanding of human learning.

The transmission notion of learning is simple and probably the "commonsense" understanding which most people have. It commonly is the notion that information constitutes understanding and that this information can be acquired by a person directly and relatively easily by listening or reading. It quite naturally leads to teaching approaches based on telling students the desired information or giving them appropriate material to read. For example, middle school students may learn that early in history an agricultural revolution occurred and people began the practice of farming as a replacement for the previously common practice of hunting and gathering. They may learn further that it resulted in a different division of labor between women and men and also between adults and children. The transmission understanding of learning is that the verbal exposition of this information, with elaboration to be sure, is the basis for students to acquire and master this new understanding.

The constructivist notion of learning is that substantial learning will not result from simple transmission, but requires a "processing" of the information by the person doing the learning. The mind is not simply a storehouse of such information. Learning results from the learner's connecting the new information to existing understandings, in many cases modifying prior understandings to accommodate the new meanings. In other words, previous knowledge gets modified in the process and associations are made between the prior understandings and the new knowledge. In our agricultural revolution illustration, for example, the learner is not simply filing the new information away in the mind as an addition to a storehouse of information but is dealing with a large set of possible connections, many of which, when brought to awareness, may challenge some prior understandings. What really is hunting and gathering? Which members of families—men, women, or children—typically did various aspects of it and why? What constitutes farming? How does it differ from hunting and gathering in terms of permanence of the family home site, and how far from such a site would members of the family typically travel? Is one activity enhanced more by a division of labor and specialization of tasks? The list of connections and potential questions goes on and on. True understanding requires processing a lot of such matters. In other words, true learning is very involved and has many facets. The learner is not a passive recipient of knowledge but is actively engaged in forming understandings or, to use the current jargon, *constructing* understanding.

This interpretation of the process of learning is relatively involved; additional explanation is in order. First, as already noted, the learner is engaged in creating meaning for him- or herself. It is a process that proceeds only with the active initiative of the learner. The construction of understanding is centered in the learner, not a teacher, computer, book, or other source of knowledge, even though all such sources may to greater or lesser degrees enhance the process in which the learner is engaged.

Second, learning is highly dependent on prior conceptions. Research shows that people generally hold many prior conceptions that are inadequate, or actually misconceptions, which must be enhanced or corrected before moving on to the intended new understandings. If hunting and gathering or farming, for example, are not well understood, or are misunderstood, the learner has work to do here before going on to dealing with an understanding of the agricultural revolution.

Third, learning is contextual. The agricultural revolution varied from one setting or context to another. The context or contexts within which the learner thinks about the matter at hand have an influence on what understandings emerge. Depending upon which of such contexts pertain, the learner's understanding may vary considerably. And the richness of the understandings the learner constructs is dependent upon the number and variability of these contexts.

Finally, learners often construct their understandings within a social setting—one in which they dialogue with others. To be sure, social constructivism is a topic that has been set aside as noted above, so clarification of what is meant here is necessary. At this point I am not talking about epistemology and what constitutes "truth." I am talking only about a mental process. Expressing one's understandings—about the agricultural revolution, for example—and listening to the statements of others foster the learning process in important ways. The social context fosters one's construction of new understandings and meanings.

Psychologists generally see learning along lines described above as constructivist. It is the understanding of learning I have and from which the discussion in this book proceeds. The transmission model is too simplistic and does not do justice to the complex mental process in which the learner is engaged. Given the overwhelming support among psychologists for this understanding of the nature of learning, one may ask why I have bothered to present it in contrast to such a simple-minded notion of learning as transmission. The reason is that we also need to address the nature of teaching, and there is an abundance of approaches to the educational process that apparently are based on a transmission notion of learning. Thus, as we discuss teaching and education activities in schools, we will need to be conscious of how we conceive of learning. In particular, we will need to be sure we are not oversimplifying the learning process and assuming that learning occurs without the student's very active participation.

## The Nature of Teaching

Discussing the nature of learning was a relatively easy task compared to laying out alternative conceptions of teaching. Teaching is practiced in many and varied ways. The form it takes is influenced not only by teacher characteristics but by a host of other factors—including the general culture, the culture of the school, economic factors, the goals favored by different segments of society, the textbooks and other materials available, and political factors. In an attempt to encompass as many factors as possible in a description of alternative conceptions of teaching, I will describe what I will call orientations of teaching. Three in number, they will carry the labels of (1) teacher-centered, (2) teacher-manager, and (3) teacher-coach, but also will be referred to by number as orientation 1, orientation 2, and orientation 3, respectively. Each will be described to a large extent in terms of three factors that vary considerably across orientations: the nature of (1) the teacher's role, (2) the students' role, and (3) the students' work.

### Orientation 1: Teacher-Centered

The process of describing this orientation makes obvious the very general nature of the three orientations, and the fact that each orientation is a broad category encompassing many variations. It also points up the fact that the teaching approach of a given teacher may not clearly and exclusively fall within one orientation. And, of course, a particular teacher may shift at times from one orientation to another, although empirical studies in classrooms suggest relatively small variation over time in the teaching orientation of a given teacher. Nevertheless, the three orientations are distinctive and quite useful to us in discussing both alternative approaches to teaching and their implications for student learning and various educational goals.

To associate orientation 1 with the transmission mode of learning would not be far off the mark; in fact, labeling this orientation as the transmission orientation to teaching could be appropriate. While many conscious users of this orientation to teaching would lay claim to a constructivist understanding of learning, the teaching approaches themselves seem to assume that simple presentation of information is the foundation of such learning. The teacher does not go much beyond such presentation to assist students in their process of constructing new understandings. The role of the teacher could be characterized as *dispenser of knowledge,* and in this role the teacher transmits information, communicates with individual students, directs student actions in laboratory or textbook exercises, and explains conceptual relationships. Although all of these roles could be expected to be part of what any teacher does—including those employing one of the other orientations—in this instance they are largely limited to purposes of dispensing knowledge. The point is that these actions constitute the essence of this orientation; little thought is given to facilitating the highly individual process of constructing understanding in which each student is engaged. The knowledge is dispensed—possibly with great clarity and enthusiasm—and students may be encouraged to engage in specific educational activities, but the internal mental processing of information by individual students largely remains beyond the consideration of the teacher.

While the reader may correctly infer from earlier statements that I favor the other orientations to teaching, it is not my intent to disparage teachers within orientation 1. It is the predominant orientation to teaching in our schools, and many teachers practice it with considerable skill, enthusiasm, and effectiveness. My basic point is that there are better alternatives, and, in fact, for certain goals a different orientation may be essential. My argument for at least sometimes using other orientations will include an argument for educational goals different from, or additional to, those currently pursued with any regularity in the schools.

To better understand how orientation 1 plays out in practice, attention must be given to the students' role and the nature of the work in which they are engaged. The student role is well described as *passive receiver* and includes recording the teacher's information, memorizing information, following teacher directions, and deferring to the teacher as the authority. The student is not the initiator, but defers to the teacher in deciding what tasks should be pursued and how information should be processed.

The student work is well described as *teacher-prescribed activities.* A typical student task would be completing a worksheet, and generally all the students will complete the same task at the same time. The teacher directs the tasks and there usually is little individualization of this work. In general, the work is marked by an *absence* of tasks that vary among students, tasks that students design or direct themselves, or tasks that emphasize reasoning or writing. Student-directed learning is not common.

## Orientation 2: Teacher-Manager

The teacher operating in this mode generally is conscious of how important student construction of their own understandings is, even though he or she may not use a label such as constructivism and may not have a well-articulated description of the process in which the student is engaged. The teacher sets out to engage students in grappling with concepts and making them their own. The role of the teacher here is well described as *manager*. The teacher helps students process information, encourages them to make connections among concepts, often communicates with them in groups where students are engaged in such "sense-making," and supervises a variety of student actions. The teacher facilitates student thinking, models the learning process by exploring new areas of understanding, and encourages flexible use of materials. The nature of the work done by students is different from that generally found in orientation 1. This difference in student work is the major distinguishing feature between the two orientations.

There also is a difference in the role of the students in this orientation. They take more responsibility for processing information, including contributing, explaining, and hypothesizing. They have more opportunity to design their own activities, rather than just follow prescribed directions from a teacher-determined activity.

Although a teacher's approach to classroom assessment and grading varies within the different orientations, there is a tendency toward particular kinds of assessment in these teaching orientations. There is a tendency for teachers in orientation 1 to use conventional teacher assignments and tests for grading purposes. Orientation number 2 generally is associated with alternative or performance-based assessment, i.e., assessment of more than just knowledge that can be displayed verbally in conventional objective or essay tests. It typically is tied to new forms of student work, including—in addition to typical tests and papers—planning documents, videotape products, work products defined by out-of-school purposes, and, in general, any product that reflects new student understanding as applied in a vast range of settings. An approach to assessment that has been gaining increasing popularity in recent years—rubric-based assessment processes—seems to be particularly compatible with this orientation. Under this approach the teacher develops a matrix which provides a careful delineation of categories describing the nature of the expected work and specific standards pertaining to varied levels of quality of this work. Although rubrics are not essential for this opening up of forms of student work, it is this change in student work that is at the heart of the reforms that generally are being sought with the use of rubrics.

While the nature of the students' work varies substantially between orientations 1 and 2, changes in the role of the student are not as dramatic. While the student has more responsibility for his or her own learning, makes choices among tasks, and has a role in designing and directing the tasks, the teacher is still the main determiner of what these tasks will be. Thus, we have the label of teacher-manager for this orientation. The teacher is the determiner of both the goals of instruction and the activities by which the goals will be pursued.

## Orientation 3: Teacher-Coach

This orientation has been given the label of teacher-coach, although the label of teacher as "personal trainer" may be more appropriate, given that the essence of this orientation is that the student plays a major role in shaping the goals of the instructional process, and in determining what activities will be pursued as a result of these personalized goals. While it may be that there are many instructional goals for which this orientation is not the optimal one, there are instructional arenas in which this orientation can be very appropriate. This may be especially true with respect to matters such as religion and spirituality, which are highly individual and personal.

The nature and role of assessment in this arena is illustrative of the situation. Because of the major change in student role under this orientation, assessment can be expected to include more student self-definition of goals and students' work products as indicators of performance. If the goals of instruction are more personal and individual, one would expect that self-assessment would play a larger role also. While some may believe that under this orientation the teacher abdicates responsibility for instruction and withdraws from the situation, it actually is a much more demanding role for the teacher. While this orientation is not limited to only a few portions of the standard instructional goals found in a school, it is particularly suitable for those that are most personal and individual.

In this context, it may be well to address the issue of what is meant by the phrase "to teach something," where this something is very personal—such as matters having a spiritual or religious dimension. The conventional meaning of this phrase is one in which the teacher determines exactly what the student should understand, think, or believe. In a public school context where the teacher does not have the responsibility of determining what the student should "believe" about spiritual or religious matters, this phrase takes on much more of the character of assisting the student in a process. The nature of the process in which students will be engaged is dependent upon their worldview, so to explore this issue in more detail, we need to turn to the matter of students' worldviews.

## Students' Worldviews

This chapter began with a discussion of educational goals. We must return to this topic again to close the chapter. My commitment is to the broad set of goals needed for a complete education. Basic skills are important but by themselves do not come close to constituting a complete education. The more in-depth approach to education reflected in the teacher-coach orientation above is particularly well-suited to some of the more sophisticated purposes in our earlier list of goals. One does not attain intellectual development, higher-order thinking skills, a positive self-concept, and moral or ethical character simply by taking in information. But using a more sophisticated teaching approach—such as the teacher-coach approach above, with its student-centered orientation—by itself does not mean that such educational goals will be attained. The content of instruction also is critical.

In particular, it is a thesis of this book that this content must give central attention to one's underlying worldview if progress is to be made in intellectual development, self-realization, career education, and moral development. The central role of worldview within a particular subject area is illustrated by the work of Cobern (1991).

But just what is a worldview? It is our assumptions about reality and truth. Sire (1997), a literary scholar, says that "A world view is a set of presuppositions (assumptions which may be true, partially true or entirely false) which we hold (consciously or subconsciously, consistently or inconsistently) about the basic make-up of the world" (p. 17). Most people assume that something exists but may not have reflected much on just what this something is nor recognized just what their assumptions are in this regard. Alternative words one might use for worldview could be "Big Picture" or "metaphysics." Huston Smith (2001), a leading scholar of world religions, uses all three of these labels interchangeably. We all have a worldview, whether or not we are aware of it or can articulate it:

> The deeper fact, however, is that to have or not have a worldview is not an option, for peripheral vision always conditions what we are attending to focally, and in conceptual "seeing" the periphery has no cutoff. The only choice we have is to be consciously aware of our worldviews and criticize them where they need criticizing, or let them work on us unnoticed and acquiesce to living unexamined lives. (Smith, 2001, p. 21)

Smith goes on to note that postmodernity "sets itself against the very idea of such a thing as the Big Picture" (p. 20), but of course, that itself is a worldview. Everyone has a set of presuppositions of what constitutes reality and gives meaning to life. Scientist and theologian John Polkinghorne and his coauthor Michael Welker (2001) make a similar point in saying that

> In the vocabulary of the scientific community, "metaphysical" often carries as pejorative a tone as does its companion word 'theological.' Yet the way in which the writers of popular books on science delight in practicing the metaphysical art (as when an author slides from science to scientism by pretending that the only questions to ask or answer are scientific) makes it clear that it is as natural to have a metaphysics as it is to speak prose. The point to strive for is adequacy to the complexity of reality, eschewing a trivial synthesis obtained through Procrustean truncation. (p. 17)

Some examples of worldviews may serve to illustrate how profoundly important the matter is. While there is a multiplicity of worldviews and they vary greatly from one person to another, a couple of common orientations are theism and naturalism. I will describe these two, as well as postmodernism, as examples. Descriptions of theism and naturalism as worldviews follow, based on the work of Sire (1997). He provides descriptions of others, such as the pantheism upon which some Eastern religions are based, but these two should meet our need here for specific illustrations.

### Theism: An Example of a Worldview

A common perspective among people in a variety of cultures has the following facets; they are persuaded that

***God exists—is personal, infinite and sovereign.*** In this view, there not only is a God, but God has personality, is infinite in power, and nothing is beyond his interest and control.

***God created the cosmos.*** While theists vary substantially in how and over what time span this occurred, there is a common conviction that it was a result of the work of God. The result is a cosmos that is orderly and not static, i.e., God is involved in the ongoing development of the universe.

***People are created in the image of God.*** The fact that people have personality is a reflection of the nature of God. They have a sense of morality, i.e., a sense of the nature of good and evil, and have a capacity for creativity, again a reflection of the nature of God.

***God communicates with people.*** God and people are in relationship. There is a capacity for communication that is exercised. God has revealed himself to people, and prayer is part of this communication.

***There is life after death.*** Death is not the extinction of personality and individuality. While there is considerable variation in theistic perspectives on life after death, they have in common the view that it is a reality.

***Ethics have their origin in the character of God.*** There is a moral dimension to life—matters of right and wrong—and God is the source of these standards. People are created in the image of God and reach their fullness when living according to these standards.

***History is linear with fulfillment of God's purpose for people.*** There is a meaningful sequence to the events of life and they have a purpose. God has purposes for the world and the choices people make have meaning for God as well as for themselves and others.

## Naturalism: An Example of a Worldview

Another common perspective in the modern age is a view that often goes under the label of *naturalism.* Within this perspective, the following are common:

***Matter exists and that is all there is.*** The cosmos itself constitutes all of reality; there is no God that transcends it.

***Personality is an outgrowth of chemical and physical properties.*** Personality is a reality, but it is an outgrowth of the interrelationships of chemical and physical properties of matter.

***Death is extinction of personality and individuality.*** At death the matter which was the foundation of this personality begins to disorganize and the personality ceases to exist.

***History is linear but has no overarching purpose.*** History is a stream of events with cause and effect but it has no particular purpose. It just is.

***Ethics are derived only from people.*** There are matters of right and wrong—good and evil—but people decide what they are. Whatever people decide they are is ethical reality.

Certainly a description of worldviews found among students in American schools would include far more than the two portrayed here, but they should serve to illustrate the dramatic difference among worldviews. It probably also is obvious that students having these two views will respond to educational activities in different ways and construct different personal meanings from them. The student who assumes that all that exists is matter potentially will construct understandings that are radically different from the person who assumes the existence of nonmaterial reality, i.e., soul or spirit. The degree of difference will depend upon the context, of course, but the potential difference is of major proportions.

Most people tend not to question their personal assumptions in this regard and rarely bring them to the fore in a conversation. But these assumptions deal with foundational views about what constitutes fundamental reality (e.g., God or the cosmos), the nature of the world around us, the nature of human beings, the purpose, if any, of life, or the nature of right or wrong. They are an articulation of how one thinks about life and the world. They are sometimes well articulated and at other times incoherent and confused, but everyone has some perspective on these matters.

## Postmodernism: Yet Another Perspective

As with other worldviews, postmodernism has numerous faces; there are many variations within this category. As a philosophical perspective—while recognizing that it also is a cultural phenomenon—it generally rejects the idea that major attention should be given to metaphysical considerations, i.e., what was previously referred to as the Big Picture or worldview, and what others have referred to as first things, foundational matters, or metanarratives. Some postmodernists recognize that we all hold some views on first things, but argue that we cannot justify them objectively—especially to other people—so we just have to live with our differences and accept that we will have a clash of faiths. Other postmodernists would argue that since we cannot establish our views on first things objectively, we should just ignore them, and if we do so they will become less important. Some persons of this persuasion argue that to focus on first things is a sign of immaturity, i.e., an attempt to justify ourselves to a higher power rather than being free, liberated, and mature. There is no predetermined purpose for life and we are liberated—free to create our own purpose. We should not make anyone or anything divine, but depend upon ourselves to establish meaning and purpose for ourselves. One could argue, of course, that this move, in effect, makes the self "divine" and the foundational beginning point for everything.

Even though people of a postmodern persuasion generally want to downplay any consideration of foundational matters or first things, it must be recognized—as noted by Smith above—that this position in itself is a worldview. Everyone faces ultimate questions about purpose, meaning, and reality at various times, and the several forms of postmodernism constitute answers to these questions, i.e., they are worldviews.

Worldviews have been portrayed here as an individual's sense of reality, but cultures also have worldviews. In fact, a primary characteristic of a culture is its worldview. One cannot understand a culture independent of its worldview.

Just how relevant is the matter of worldview to a student's education? It is a major thesis of this book that it is central and essential. A "complete" education extends well beyond those cognitive matters that can be judged "correct" or "incorrect" in a factual information sense, and includes a host of matters in which there is a strong interaction between "simple" cognitive matters and matters of values and personal commitments. A complete education in many areas is not possible without attention to one's worldview. To expect a student to consider many issues (e.g., many sociopolitical or personal-choice issues) on bases that exclude all "religious" aspects of one's worldview is to de facto impose on the student a form of indoctrination.

While one's worldview may not be all that consistent, it does tend to be relatively stable. It certainly is subject to change but such changes are slow in coming. And this process of shaping and developing one's personal worldview is central to the educational process. It is not the purpose of public education to foist on anyone a particular worldview, although one purpose should be to help students clarify their understanding of their worldview, consider alternatives, reflect on inconsistencies in their perspectives, and understand the implications of their worldview for how they will live their lives.

A complete education is not possible without personal engagement and commitment (or informed suspended judgment) regarding many issues. To limit an education to those matters which can be addressed as objectively "true" or "false" is to provide a seriously truncated education.

One's worldview is intimately related to one's life commitments. Thus, unless one expects that a student's education should be passionless and devoid of attention to one's commitments, students' worldviews have to come into the picture. As a result, this chapter closes with the summary contention that (1) a broad range of educational goals is appropriate and necessary for public education, (2) a more in-depth orientation to teaching—such as orientation 3—is essential at least at some points in the educational process, and (3) at many such points the student needs to attend to his or her worldview.

In the next chapter we will examine more closely the potential role of religion and spirituality in this complete education. If an education is complete, to what extent must or should religion and spirituality play a part? In a later chapter we will return to the topic of students' worldviews and their connection to their personal spirituality and religious perspectives.

# THREE

## *Religion and Spirituality in a Complete Education*

What is the role of religion and spirituality in a complete education? To discuss this role, it is essential to have an understanding of what religion and spirituality are, but acquiring common definitions for our use here is not easy, since the words are used in so many different ways. Sorting them out, however, is worth the effort.

### What Are Spirituality and Religion?

#### Spirituality

We will begin with spirituality. Many people think of spirituality in the sense in which it is defined by McGrath:

> Spirituality concerns the quest for a fulfilled and authentic religious life, involving the bringing together of the ideas distinctive of that religion and the whole experience of living on the basis of and within the scope of that religion. (McGrath, 1999, p. 2)

From this perspective, religion and spirituality are intertwined. While this integration of spirituality and religion probably is a predominant view, a popular expression today is "I am spiritual but not religious." Some people are convinced of a spiritual reality and consider it an important aspect of their life, but do not think of it in a religious sense.

In her book, *The Soul of Education*, Rachael Kessler approaches spirituality in public education from a nonreligious perspective:

> If we define spirituality in terms of beliefs that one group holds and others do not, we violate the First Amendment by imposing such beliefs through curriculums in public schools. It is true that for many adults, spirituality is inextricably linked with their particular faith and doctrines. Listening to students for many years, however, has shown me that young people have experiences that nourish their spiritual development and *yet are not directly related to worldview or religious dogma*. We *can* honor the First Amendment without abandoning our children's spiritual development. (Kessler, 2000, p. xiv)

Kessler apparently wishes to define spirituality in this limited sense (i.e., with worldview and religious belief considerations excluded), at least partially out of a fear of imposing beliefs upon students. She wishes to include spirituality in the curriculum in a fairly pervasive manner without fear of raising First Amendment issues. Her book provides excellent resources for someone undertaking such an approach. At the same time that she is emphasizing the importance of teachers in a public school not espousing spiritual beliefs, she also emphasizes that "the First Amendment protects the rights of our children to *freely express their own beliefs.*" While her approach has much to commend it, I find it, by itself, inadequate for the purposes at hand because for many students spirituality in its full sense is—as she says it is for many adults—"inextricably linked with their particular faith and doctrines." In effect, she faces the potential hazard of imposing on students an understanding of spirituality which *excludes* a religious dimension. While appreciating her educational endeavors, her stance illustrates for me the dilemma we face at every turn when addressing the role of religion in public education. By including it, you run the risk of imposing beliefs that violate the First Amendment. By excluding religious perspectives, however, you also run the risk of imposing a view of reality which implies the nonexistence, or at least irrelevance, of religion other than as a cultural phenomenon.

For purposes of this book, our definition of spirituality must include the *potential* for a religious component. It will be up to individual students to determine in what sense matters of spirituality include for them a religious understanding. Thus, no particular definition of spirituality has been selected from the highly varied ones in common usage to focus our attention here. When the term is used here it is expected to encompass definitions as open as "personal response to the mystery of the world" (Raymo, 1998) and as specific as ones embedded in a particular religious system.

## Religion

Religion gives us definitional problems also. Broadly defined, "religion is about the relationship between human beings and the supernatural world" (Levinson, 1996, p. vii). Levinson goes on to use the term *religious system* "to mean all of the shared religious beliefs and practices that comprise the human-supernatural relationship of a particular indigenous culture or a particular world religion" (Levinson, 1996, p. vii). But we need more detail in our definition if it is to be helpful to us in our consideration of educational issues.

There is a tendency to equate religion with beliefs, dogma, or worldview. While beliefs generally are an important part of religion, a definition centered exclusively upon beliefs actually perpetuates misconceptions about the nature of religion. In an attempt to portray religion in a more complete sense, it will be described here in terms of three aspects: (1) beliefs, (2) "doing," and (3) "being."

If asked to describe their religion, a large percentage of people would begin with a description of key beliefs. A Christian, for example, probably would begin with a discussion of a belief in God, the incarnation of Jesus of Nazareth, and the presence of the Holy Spirit. An adherent of a different religion would present different beliefs, but in the great majority of cases these beliefs would have central prominence.

The second component, labeled here as "doing," is the arena of action. Whether these actions are in the area of the personal, social, or political, they probably are considered to be a significant component of a given religion. Religions vary in the relative importance attached to beliefs and actions, and the way in which they relate to each other, but it would be rare for both not to have importance.

In many people's minds, the third component, "being," has to do with an individual's moral or ethical character. Others may describe it in more mystical terms, or in terms of an ongoing personal relationship with God. While probably not the first aspect mentioned by someone asked to define their religion, it commonly is a part of someone's religious understandings.

A definition narrower than this three-dimensional one is inadequate for a discussion of the role of religion in public education because all three are important to many religious people. Whether the context is an academic discussion of the role of a particular religion in world history, or listening to a student's personal expression of religious convictions, a teacher with an understanding of religion that does not include the potential for all three dimensions is unlikely to comprehend all that is relevant.

***Worldview.*** Without diminishing the importance of the other two components in our definition of religion, it must be granted that the beliefs component is particularly central to any discussion of religion in education. For individuals with theistic beliefs, these beliefs are integral to their worldview, Big Picture, or metaphysics. One's religious perspective is part of one's understanding of reality. Only the most shallow and impersonal form of education could avoid touching upon such a student's worldview, or for that matter, one with an atheistic worldview. As noted in the previous chapter, having or not having a worldview is not an option. They are part of who we are. We do have a choice, of course, about consciously developing an understanding of where we have grounded our understanding of reality and the choices we are making as a result of this understanding. Whether it is vaguely understood or well articulated, everyone has a worldview.

Worldviews can vary dramatically. One student, for example, may have a theistic worldview that assumes a spiritual reality, the existence of God, ethics that are derived from God's revelation, and a purpose to life and history. In contrast, another student may have a naturalistic worldview in which atoms and molecules constitute all of reality, ethics are a human construct, and life has no discernible purpose. Yet another student may have a more postmodern worldview into which any metanarrative at all is rejected. And, of course, there are any number of other worldviews as well. But to make Huston Smith's (2001) point again, everyone has a worldview. Furthermore, a nontrivial education is impossible without attention to the worldview held by a student.

## The Centrality of Religion and Spirituality in a Complete Education

The role of religion in education has caught the attention of an increasing number of academics during the last decade. More and more, there is a recognition that education is both incomplete and distorted if religion is left out of the picture. Perhaps due to either real or perceived dilemmas posed by the First Amendment, religion has been avoided in the past. Some would argue that this recent increased attention has led to important changes in at least some areas of the curriculum. It is said that the typical world history curriculum in schools today gives greater recognition to the role of religion than the curriculum did just a decade ago. Ascertaining whether these changes are major or minor would be difficult to substantiate at this point, but at least the issue is more recognized now.

Academics have approached the issue from a variety of perspectives. James W. Fraser (1999), for example, has argued from a multicultural perspective that attention to religion is essential. Based on a careful historical and philosophical analysis of the American experience, along with an "insider's" understanding of the nature of a religiously based life, his work grapples with the educational issues and penetrates to the essence of what is involved for students.

Others, such as Nash (1999) and Noddings (1993), concentrate major attention on the belief aspects of religion and approach their work primarily from a philosophical perspective. Although both Noddings and Nash seem to focus on the first of the three aspects of religion presented above—namely, belief—they also seem to want to judge the value of a belief by its results—at least in a collective sense. So, they do attend to "doing" somewhat, but, in the main, they do not really grapple with the place of the personal "doing" and "being" aspects of a religion in the educational context.

The most comprehensive treatment of the topic probably is that of Warren A. Nord (1995), who has done a detailed analysis of the status of religion in American education and made specific proposals of steps that can be taken within public education to give religion a more appropriate place. In terms of the practical world of schooling, a smaller book coauthored by Nord with Charles Haynes (1998) is quite specific in how religion can be addressed across the curriculum.

This increased attention to religion and spirituality also is evidenced in governmental action. In 1995, the Clinton administration's Secretary of Education, Richard W. Riley, issued a set of guidelines for educators (an updated version with slight modifications was issued in May 1998) that spelled out in considerable detail the manner in which religion should be addressed in the public schools of America. It included curricular matters, students' expression of personal convictions, teachers' personal religious perspectives, and school policies. A similar statement was issued by the subsequent Bush administration. In both of the academic analyses mentioned above and these governmental actions, there is evidence of growing recognition that ignoring or eliminating religion leads to an incomplete and distorted education. This increased attention to religion within public education is encouraging and is a backdrop for the discussions in this book. (For a statement from the First Amendment Center that summarizes current policies on these matters see the appendix.

## The Dilemma

Earlier in this chapter reference was made to the central dilemma encountered when addressing the role of religion in public education. By including it in an inappropriate manner, one runs the risk of imposing beliefs in violation of the First Amendment. By limiting religious perspectives, however, one risks imposing a view of reality which implies the nonexistence, or at least irrelevance, of religion other than as a cultural phenomenon. In essence, it can become schooling grounded in a worldview of secularism. A contrast drawn by Marcus Borg (1999) is helpful in grasping this situation. While noting that there are a multitude of worldviews, he points out that

> broadly speaking, worldviews fall into two main categories: religious and secular. For a secular worldview, there is only "this"—and by "this" I mean the visible world of our ordinary experience. For a religious worldview, there is "this" and "more than this." The "more than this" has been variously named, imaged, and conceptualized. I will simply call it "the sacred." A religious worldview sees reality as grounded in the sacred. For a secular worldview, there is no sacred ground. (p. 9)

Thus, our dilemma, as viewed from one side of the divide: If religious students are asked to engage in a process of schooling that is grounded entirely in the secular, they are being asked to conduct their thinking to a considerable extent as if their understanding of reality is wrong.

For the student with some form of a religious worldview, the result can sometimes become quite difficult, alienating, and stifling. If the ground rules of the school culture—whether explicit or tacit—call for matters of religious reality to be left unspoken or privatized, the religious student is being asked to be inauthentic, less than a complete person, and to stand outside the mainstream of the school.

## Examples of Inadequate Solutions to the Dilemma

Many solutions have been proposed to the dilemma at hand. On the one hand, it is common to hear among some members of the public an outcry for a "return" to including the specific teaching of specific religious perspectives in the school curricula. For lack of a better label, we may call this a religious fundamentalist approach to education. It tends to be separatist and exclusivist in nature. In spite of what an adequate historical understanding would convey to us—and in spite of the concerns of a very diverse and pluralistic population—some groups continue to press for daily Bible reading in the schools, public prayers, the posting of the Ten Commandments, and related actions focused on specific religious persuasions.

This outlook often seems to be correlated with a preference for a limited curriculum—a desire for a curriculum that includes little attention to values or personal development—apparently in fear of perspectives being taught that may deviate from rather specific doctrines. There is an obvious reluctance to accept educational pluralism or the secular orientation of some students. This perspective has been debated extensively in the public square over the last few decades, and its rejection and inadequacies have been well covered in the public press.

While the need to reject this viewpoint may seem obvious to the educated reader, there is another "fundamentalist" position whose inadequacies may not be so obvious. There is a secular perspective which also is separatist and exclusivist in nature. Often tied to a naturalistic worldview, there is a desire for education without reference to the religious, apparently based on the assumption that secular viewpoints are all that are relevant in education and life. As with religious fundamentalism, there is a desire for a limited curriculum, one devoid of anything that might be thought of as a "spiritual reality" or worldviews that treat religion as anything other than a cultural phenomenon. As with our prior example, there is a reluctance to accept educational pluralism or accommodate the needs of students with other viewpoints.

## Is There a Solution?

I am convinced there is a solution to our dilemma—a solution that does not just avoid the two extreme positions portrayed above, but one which truly responds to the educational needs of all students. Such a solution must attend to the nature of learning and teaching, as well as a wide range of educational objectives as described in the previous chapter. This solution has two main facets in addition to the simple inclusion of religious content in appropriate parts of the curriculum, such as world history: (1) incorporating appropriate and adequate attention to worldviews in the curriculum, such as when addressing the nature of research in different academic fields, and (2) providing opportunities for individual students' integration of their understandings across fields of study and at the intersect of competing worldviews.

Further attention to these matters must take into account the context of American education and the nature of the schooling conducted there. These matters will be addressed in the next chapter, after which we can return to dealing directly with our dilemma.

# FOUR
## *The American Educational Context*

Thus far we have considered the nature of a complete education and the role of religion and spirituality within it. While the structure and general nature of American schooling have been mentioned at times, they have not been given detailed attention. Nevertheless, the American educational context—its society, culture, and politics, and the schools which are an outgrowth of them—is centrally relevant to our discussion. We now turn attention to this context.

### A Brief Historical Sketch

At the time the original colonies were established in the New World, of course, there was no system of public education, even within the individual colonies. It was an unorganized collection of informal arrangements in which schooling was provided by families, private tutors, and other catch-as-catch-can arrangements. The main goal was basic literacy—the ability to read, write, and do basic arithmetic. The underlying purposes were very utilitarian, but also religious, i.e., to be able to read the Bible. But rather quickly, organized approaches to education emerged. In 1647 a law in Massachusetts mandated that any town reaching a size of 50 households had to appoint someone in the town to teach all children to read and write. Similar moves were made in other colonies as time went on.

After nationhood, education was still a state matter. Even without a national system, however, quite common patterns emerged across the nation. By the mid-1800s the "common school" movement had taken hold with the often-cited influence of Horace Mann being particularly important. The religious rationale for such education was still significant and the materials used for instruction prominently featured aspects of the dominant religion of the area—essentially some form of Protestantism. The quite sectarian approaches of the original separate colonies had evolved into a common approach that featured the more generic aspects of Protestantism. This dominance of Protestantism, along with increased immigration of Catholics from Europe, led to the development of substantial numbers of private Catholic schools across the country.

The commitment of Catholic communities in the nineteenth century to establish private schools alongside the public schools—at great expense—is illustrative of the tensions over religion in the schools. The issues have changed over the decades—with some recurring—but the tensions persist to the present. Because of these tensions within a pluralistic nation, the general tendency has been to eliminate many of the public school features that led to the tensions in the first place, with the result that schools have become quite secular places. The evolution of a common school system has led to schools in which religion is not as prominent as it is in the larger society.

## The General Cultural Context

It goes without saying that the general cultural context of the United States is characterized by diversity and pluralism. As the United States enters the twenty-first century, it is more diverse than it has ever been culturally, ethnically, and religiously, as well as in terms of the ethical norms to which people expect to adhere within our society. One does not need to search far to find pockets of both religious fervor and secular approaches to life:

> At the dawn of the new millennium the peoples of the United States are more secular, especially in their public culture, more religious, in many different private forms, and more diverse than ever before in the nation's history. (Fraser, 1999, p. 4)

During the past century our understanding of religious diversity has changed greatly. While America was once thought of as largely Christian—with diversity within this category in terms of Catholicism and various forms of Protestantism, and a significant but small Jewish minority—the situation today is far more diverse. The Muslim population is now said to be larger than the Jewish population; Buddhist and Hindu people are commonplace; and a variety of other faith commitments can be found. And it also must be recognized that many people who think of themselves as secular have a conception of reality which also leads to a commitment to a particular way of life. Although based on a secular worldview, it is a commitment to a pattern of living analogous to the commitments others ground in their religious beliefs.

Given this diversity and the centrality of religious commitments to many people's way of life, it is not surprising that we hear much discussion of "cultural wars" in our society. These disagreements are reflected in the general media, radio talk shows, political fund-raising, and various forms of political activism. In other words, we not only have diversity, we have conflicts that result from this diversity.

All of this is related to the American understanding of democracy. We expect that our democratic approach to government and public discourse will accommodate this diversity and its resultant conflicts. Since public education is an integral part of this democratic way of life, we must expect that this diversity and conflict will extend into the school context and that our democratic approaches will allow us to accommodate in a reasonable manner both the religious and nonreligious orientations to life of various students and their parents.

## The Academic Cultural Context

The academic culture, i.e., the culture of higher education and in particular the research-oriented universities, is an important influence on both American culture generally and K-12 public education. To more adequately understand the academic culture, it is important to look at its organization into various disciplines and at the epistemologies—or ways of acquiring new understandings—that characterize these disciplines. The typical university is organized into departments along disciplinary lines, resulting in departments of physics, history, fine arts, philosophy, literature, mathematics, and so forth. While such disciplines differ in terms of the focus or subject of study, they also differ in terms of the research methodologies employed. While the methodologies employed within a given discipline may vary considerably, there tend to be even larger differences across the methodologies employed in these many disciplines.

Because of this departmentalization of research activities, relatively little attention is given to the integration of knowledge across such disciplines. In other words, one's overall worldview or metaphysics tends not to be prominent in the intellectual activities of researchers in a given department. The only department explicitly committed to the integration of understandings across such boundary lines is the field of philosophy, but even here the focus often is on subquestions rather than the Big Picture.

A valuable example is found in the natural sciences in such areas as evolutionary biology and cosmology. The methodologies of scientific investigation operate on the assumptions that there is uniformity in nature and that data should be acquired only by sensory means. No spiritual reality is assumed; in fact, it is explicitly excluded as a possible consideration in the work of the natural sciences. Thus, when addressing questions about the origins of the universe and of life, the researcher is operating from what might be thought of as a naturalistic worldview. Yet, even though this is the operating approach, many of the same scientists have a personal worldview that is different. Methodological naturalism is not the same as philosophical or epistemological naturalism. Survey data tells us that approximately 40 percent—a number that has been relatively stable for decades—of biologists and physicists believe in a personal God and pray. Obviously, the worldview under which they live their lives and understand reality is not the same as the operational methodologies employed in their professional work. This is not a surprising, disconcerting, or problematic situation. Each of these persons is, to a lesser or greater extent, integrating understandings from various arenas in their overall approach to life. What is important to note about the general academic culture, however, is that such integrating of understandings is assumed to be a personal matter and not something deserving of much public discourse. While this may be a satisfactory approach within the context at hand, we will see that it has implications we must address when we turn to our discussion of the teaching of evolution in schools.

## Postmodernism

The topic at hand demands that we attend to a matter that is both a cultural phenomenon and an academic movement—postmodernism. A term not well understood by the general public, it is descriptive of both important trends within the general culture and approaches to scholarly understanding within the academic world. As the word itself indicates, it marks the end of commitment to the modern outlook of objectivity and rationality. All understandings are not an outgrowth of objective reality and they are not strictly dependent upon rational analysis. The emotions and personal interpretations are important parts of the picture. This general cultural outlook is reflected in literature, films, music, and architecture. Postmodernism is a general cultural phenomenon as well as an academic outlook.

As philosopher, Stanley Grenz (1996) has said, "Postmodernism defies definitive description" (p. 40). Because it rejects the assumption of an objective world—and a belief that human rationality can bring us to an understanding of this objective reality—we are in a setting with a multiplicity of outlooks and personal interpretations. It honors diversity and as such is an outlook for a diverse and pluralistic society. The same is true in the academic world as well, where diversity of all types is honored and postmodern perspectives have gained prominence through the work of such scholars as Derrida, Foucault, and Rorty.

The movement has been from an *objectivist* outlook to a *constructivist* outlook, but in saying so I need to note that I am here using the word *constructivist* in a different sense than in our earlier discussion of human learning where reference was made to cognitive or psychological constructivism. In the earlier instance the point of discussion was how learning occurs in the mind. In this case the word is used in a more philosophical sense to describe a view of what constitutes knowledge. In the postmodern view, knowledge is more a human construct than a reflection of an objective reality. As one homespun philosopher (with tongue in cheek?) has said about the academic world, "Academe is committed to the search for truth, as long as you don't think you have found it."

Reference was made earlier to certain general cultural wars. Analogous conflicts occur within the academic world. For example, reference is often made to "the science wars," a conflict which reaches to the roots of scholars' understanding of the nature of science and the development of scientific knowledge. Scientists generally hold to a realist notion of knowing—at least as an operating principle for their work—and there have been vociferous—and sometimes vitriolic—debates between some of them and scholars in the field of scientific studies about the nature of science and what constitutes science knowledge. An in-depth discussion of this topic is beyond the scope of this book, but it deserves mention because it bears upon some of the conflicts at hand and the approach we may take to religion and spirituality in the curriculum of the public schools.

## The Two Cultures

Given the several cultural or academic "wars" which seem to be portrayed as battles between two well-defined sides, it is not surprising that some observers perceive a divide between two different cultures in America. Noted scholar Gertrude Himmelfarb (1999), for example, has written a book about American society whose title includes the phrase, "Two Cultures." Her analysis is sophisticated and nuanced and does not fall into oversimplified "either/or" thinking that forces everything into one of two categories. Nevertheless, she shows two general tendencies on a variety of matters which tend to cluster together at one pole or the other.

While her analysis does not portray these two cultures as one being religious and the other nonreligious, there is more of a tendency toward formal religion in one and a tendency toward more secularly derived ethics and norms in the other. Although her work may not be of central importance to this book, there is a sense in which it helps to understand the educational issues at hand. The dilemma of how to deal with religion and spirituality in the public school curriculum is not just an educational debate. It reflects a tendency generally toward tension over how people's religion will be visible in public life and the extent to which it is public or private.

In another scholarly analysis, Stephen L. Carter (1993) has addressed the tension between, on the one hand, a dominant culture which omits a religious perspective—as reflected in the title of his book, *The Culture of Disbelief*—and, on the other hand, the personal and often private outlook of a large portion of the populace which gives a central place to matters of religion and spirituality. Carter, a law professor, has examined the issue largely from a legal perspective and gives major attention to educational issues brought to the courts.

Granted that these differing cultural perspectives are vying for places of prominence in our culture and the curriculum of the schools, the issue at hand is not simply the multicultural one of giving all cultures their due and allowing all students to benefit from the contributions of many cultures in addition to their own. The issue extends to matters of worldview, metaphysics, and the need for an intellectual education which is not provincial and limited to certain cultural perspectives. Furthermore, it is a matter of each student being able to grapple with these issues in a variety of contexts and direct their own intellectual development in a manner that results in an integrated intellectual outlook which is foundational both to their personal development and whatever further education they pursue.

### Worldview and Postmodernism

There is a lot of disagreement among scholars as to just what postmodernism entails, but there is agreement that it marks the end of the domination of one worldview as the universal one. The Enlightenment project with its commitment to objective reality and rational understandings is not the only game in town; in fact, some would claim its demise is certain. Postmodernism is a commitment to a plurality of interpretations, but not surprisingly, some would claim that if you carry this outlook to its logical conclusion you end up in a logical contradiction: by rejecting all "metanarratives" or coherent "Big Pictures" of reality, you are in effect enshrining a new "Big Picture," one in which everything is relative.

Without pursuing more of that particular debate, it is appropriate to return here to a point made earlier: Everyone has a worldview. It may not be a metanarrative of the kind that postmodernists insist on rejecting, but it is some personal understanding of reality and how one knows it. It is a foundation for one's actions and commitments. Education that ignores this situation is bound to be impersonal and incomplete.

Within our postmodern culture, there is a suspicion of universal answers to the existential questions of life; thus, there is a suspicion of orthodoxies and any approach to education that is authoritarian or seeks to impose any dogma on students. A related phenomenon is a suspicion of formal religion in the public arena. When it comes to matters of religion, the tendency is to say in response to any expression of religious conviction, "That's great for you," or "Whatever." It also is related to an expression heard with increasing frequency: "I'm spiritual, but not religious."

All of this is part of the dilemma we face in addressing matters of religion and spirituality in public education. On the one hand, matters of religion and spirituality are an important part of the lives of great numbers of people and education is seriously incomplete when it is ignored. But the diversity of this religion and spirituality constrains how it can be addressed. This dilemma must remain in mind as we probe more deeply into the context of American education.

## The Nature of Mass Schooling

Schooling and education are not the same thing. While ideally one would hope that formal schooling would result in authentic education, the connection is not always so direct. The barriers to mass schooling reaching its goals are many, not the least of which is the constraint of economics. Schooling must be done on a mass basis for economic reasons. The idea of one-on-one instruction between a teacher and student may be a valued ideal, but in practical economic terms it obviously is impossible. Whatever teacher-student ratio is in place, whether that be one teacher and a class of twenty students, or one teacher with a class of forty students, it is a less-than-perfect compromise.

We are stuck with mass education as an economic necessity. On the other hand, the character of our mass education is not always determined by economic necessity. Particular educational approaches in a given school setting may be the result of philosophical commitments, the entrenchments of certain educational traditions, or simply a reluctance to reflect upon and challenge current practices.

When considering new approaches to religion in public education, we will need to acknowledge all of the factors that lead to large classes, educational approaches consistent with mass education, and the general tendency to impersonalize education as a result of its mass nature. Many aspects of the reforms advocated in this book can be practiced quite readily within the overall pattern of mass education to which we have become accustomed; other aspects will require a more extensive rethinking of our approach to mass education. In either case, the intent is to pursue reforms that are viable within the constraints of currently allocated resources. I am advocating reforms of fundamental importance that are professionally challenging—but economically viable.

In taking these steps, it will be especially important to address our purposes for education and rethink what it means to be an educated person and to attain that goal in public education. In addition, it is important to recognize that in spite of their prominence in political and educational discussions, in the "real world" of schools, diversity and pluralism are addressed only incompletely. We will need to address what it means to take them seriously—including our religious pluralism, not just our ethnic and cultural pluralism.

## The Current Role of Religion in U.S. Education

A number of references and allusions to the inappropriately low level of attention to religion and spirituality in U.S. public education already have been made in this book. One indication of the validity of this general view was the perceived need by the Clinton administration to issue a set of guidelines on the role of religion in American public education (Riley, 1998). The gaps between these guidelines and apparent contemporary educational practice—as well as the apparent surprise on the part of many educators when faced with the content of these guidelines—all point to the relatively low level of extant attention to religious matters in public education. After passage of the No Child Left Behind legislation in 2002, the Bush administration issued guidelines similar to those of the Clinton administration that included reference to penalties imposed by the new legislation for schools that failed to comply with the guidelines.

I will return to this point in the context of specific case studies of educational practice in later chapters, but some particular examples will be helpful at this point to establish context. In general there is a de facto preference for secular rather than religious outlooks when addressing any aspect of the curriculum in public education, even though the topic at hand may be of a religious nature. For example, during the past Christmas season an elementary school teacher decided to have a Christmas celebration in her class that was focused only upon a secularized Santa Claus with an explicit omission of anything with a religious character. When some Christian fundamentalist parents decided to keep their daughter home from school on the day of the celebration, she could not comprehend their concern. As far she was concerned she was following the letter of the law in omitting any religious references and had no apparent comprehension that she was, in fact, radically changing the meaning of Christmas for this girl as she understood it and imposing a different cultural perspective in its place. She did not recognize her lack of sensitivity to the concerns of the student, nor did she understand what a multicultural approach to education would mean. A hegemony of secular over religious outlooks was in place. It must be granted that this teacher was facing a true dilemma that needed to be resolved. On the other hand, resolving the dilemma may not have been as difficult as it appeared on the surface. It is such dilemmas that need our attention.

But it also must be recognized that the dilemmas we face are far more complex than portrayed in this specific example. We must get beyond them to address more underlying worldview issues found throughout the curriculum and what it takes to provide a complete education for students in which all aspects of their personal development are taken into account, even though all of them may not be addressed in their totality.

## The Limitations of Current Practice

As already noted, a complete education that includes a religious dimension is difficult to attain in the public arena as a result of the large numbers of students to be served and the pluralistic context. But there are abundant indications that the degree of incompleteness is greater than it needs to be. Thus, it seems profitable to examine in more detail limitations of current practice that underlie this incompleteness.

### Compartmentalization

Among the reasons current educational practice tends toward incompleteness and lack of comprehensiveness is the compartmentalization of knowledge. Scholarly work tends to be pursued within the confines of academic disciplines. Likewise, the presentation of information in an educational context also tends to be compartmentalized within the same disciplines. As a result, there is a tendency to assume the epistemological foundations of the given discipline—i.e., the methods of scholarly inquiry within that discipline—as a pervasive epistemology that can in some senses substitute for a more broad-based worldview held by a particular individual. In general, the tendency is to avoid addressing the worldview aspects and simply operate within the confines of a particular discipline or compartment. For example, with respect to education in the natural sciences, whether in secondary education or higher education, there generally is some tendency to address aspects of the nature of science, though probably not in great depth. It would be rare, however, for such instruction to give significant attention to the nature of science as it relates to other ways of knowing. Such intellectual exploration tends to stop at the boundaries of the discipline.

In some academic circles there has been some tendency in recent years to address the interface of science and religion, as evidenced by numerous conferences and publications. Within the confines of formal education, however, serious attention to this interface is rarely found. To a considerable extent, the neglect of this interface is a by-product of the compartmentalization of knowledge.

A further reason for its neglect is a failure of teacher education to address such matters. The compartmentalization of the traditional disciplines is assumed and little attempt is made to move beyond it.

### Lack of Integration

Another feature of current educational practice is the absence of attention to the integration of knowledge across disciplines. Although it might be said to be a by-product of the compartmentalization just discussed above, this lack of integration actually is a somewhat separate matter, since in principle there is no reason that educational practice could not focus upon integration across the boundaries of the disciplines. It is rarely done in actual practice, even though it occasionally is recommended on a more theoretical level. For example, the integration of science and mathematics instruction has frequently been advocated, as well as the integration of history and literature. In spite of its place in the educational literature for many decades, it is rarely found in actual school practice.

If this type of integration were pursued, there is reason to think that the epistemological basis of each of these fields of necessity would receive more attention. It would not be as easy to blithely assume an epistemology, and there would be more reason for matters of worldview to come to the fore. Integration across fields probably would lead to more attention to epistemological matters.

## Neglected Applications of Knowledge

There is a general tendency in American educational practice to give relatively minor consideration to the applications of knowledge in a given field. Possibly as a result of a heavy commitment within the school culture to the "preparation ethic"—i.e., preparation for the next level of schooling, such as preparation of high school students for college—instruction focused upon the application of disciplinary knowledge to societal issues or personal concerns typically gets relatively low attention in the classroom.

Some educators argue that the need for an adequate education in the basics of the various disciplines is so great—and the need for time and other resources so large—that there is insufficient time to address the applications of knowledge. This viewpoint reflects values that give disciplinary knowledge the highest priority and allot little time for its applications. There is a counterargument that gives high priority to disciplinary knowledge but demands attention to the applications of this knowledge as well. For example, it can be argued on the basis of the nature of learning that a variety of applications of any particular knowledge should be taught not only for their own sake, but also for the sake of more in-depth understanding of the knowledge itself. The creation of understanding is fostered by attending to it in a variety of contexts.

If, in fact, the applications of knowledge were given more serious attention across the disciplines, connecting this knowledge to religion would be easier and more obviously of need. Any educational reforms regarding religion are closely related to general educational reform endeavors.

## Curricular Imbalance

Within current educational practice there is a curricular imbalance, in the sense that religion does not receive the attention it deserves. This topic has received considerable attention during the past decade, and it is fairly well documented. The Association for Supervision and Curriculum Development (ASCD) publication *Taking Religion Seriously across the Curriculum*, by Nord and Haynes (1998), provides good documentation of this point. They point to numerous examples—such as insufficient attention to religion in world history—in building a general case of this curricular imbalance. This curricular imbalance is not the only reason current practice is limited, but if this matter were addressed appropriately, it would go a long way toward solving our problem.

This problem is exacerbated by the lack of appropriate instructional materials that give the appropriate attention to religious matters. Furthermore, teacher education generally does not prepare teachers well to address these matters on their own. The desired resources apparently are in low supply.

## Impersonal Education

Education tends to be impersonal for many reasons, not the least of which is the large number of students with whom the teacher is faced. But the reasons go beyond large numbers. There is a reluctance on the part of teachers to be too personal, especially in the total class context. Teachers often fear it for a variety of reasons, including concerns about invading students' privacy, being misunderstood, or being thought to have committed some impropriety. Teachers often think of themselves as not having the skills for entry into the personal arena; counselors are thought to be the professionals with these skills. Finally, teachers may not think it is important. The academic basics are thought to be the particular goal of education, and more personal aspects belong somewhere else. It is easy to see why—with such an impersonal orientation to education—religious matters would have relatively low priority, aside from any consideration of First Amendment issues.

## Lack of Student Empowerment and Individual Choice

Public education generally is not an arena within which students have much empowerment or individual choice. The curriculum of the schools is largely determined in a top-down fashion without significant student input. The style in which education is pursued within a given class is largely teacher determined. Again, we have indications of how impersonal public education tends to be, yet individual choice is necessary if religion is to get its due. Students must be empowered to make at least some curricular decisions, obviously within predetermined bounds. Some aspects of a complete education obviously are personal, and formal schooling must make provision for students to individually pursue these aspects. A cookie-cutter, one-choice-fits-all approach to education is inadequate. While there are many other reasons why individual student choice is essential for an authentic education, giving religion its due is one of them.

### Addressing the Dilemma

The dilemma is real. Having a complete education that encompasses multiple objectives and is truly personal and individual is not easy in our public education setting. As noted above, the public context has many constraints, including large student-teacher ratios and its pluralistic context. The limitations of current practice are significant, and there are many factors that make it difficult to bring about significant change. What then is the answer to our dilemma?

The most common answer to the dilemma is to modify current practice to incorporate more attention to religion and spirituality. With respect to religion, this case has been made well by, among others, Nord (1995) and Nord and Haynes (1998). Much can and should be done, as they have so ably stated. But we also should ask whether or not these modifications of current school practices are truly enough. Or is it necessary to rethink the very essence of the educational process? Is it really possible to give religion and spirituality their due without reconceptualizing the educational process?

It is my contention that what these authors are advocating is good and appropriate, but by itself is insufficient. More fundamental changes will be necessary if enough attention is to be given to the alternative worldviews held by various students and if there is to be sufficient allowance for varied viewpoints among individual students to enable them to foster their own education in a manner compatible with their personal religiosity and spirituality. The personal element needs a bigger place. To address this point more seriously, however, we must explore in depth what constitutes the curriculum of the schools. That is the subject of the next chapter.

# FIVE

# *The Curriculum*

To consider the possibility of fundamental changes in the school program that go beyond simply adding more content about religion, we need to explore the nature of the curriculum itself. It is a bigger topic than it may appear on the surface because it brings us face-to-face with the nature of education—not just the nature of schooling, but of education itself.

The commonsense understanding of the word *curriculum* is much like that of the dictionary definition, a course of study or the subjects to be taught. But curriculum is a rich word and it can include additional understandings. Most definitions of curriculum at least start with identification of certain knowledge which is to be taught, but additional facets must be included if alternative visions of the curriculum are to be understood. In addition to identifying the knowledge itself, one must have an understanding of why it is worthy of pursuit.

For example, if one were studying a nineteenth-century American novel simply for the sake of the pleasure of reading it, one probably would approach it quite differently than if the intent were to gain a deeper understanding of the culture of that day. Certainly, literature classes could read such a novel with both purposes in mind, but nevertheless the point is still valid: Why certain content is included in the curriculum influences how it will be pursued. The study of mathematics will be pursued differently if the intent is to gain practical, everyday computational skills than if the intent is to understand the nature of mathematics. Similarly, the study of microorganisms will be pursued differently depending upon whether the reason for studying them is simply to understand them for their own sake, to apply this knowledge to personal health, and/or to understand the nature of scientific investigations.

Our understanding of curriculum depends not only upon *why* we are interested in particular content but *how* we intend to pursue our knowledge of it. What a student gains from a lecture about a novel is different from what is gained by a small group of readers discussing with each other their personal reactions to the novel. What a student gains from a session practicing particular mathematical computational *skills* is different from an exploration of alternative ways of mathematical *problem solving*. What a student gains from reading about microorganisms is different from that gained from pursuing open-ended questions about microorganisms through laboratory investigations. What a student gains from reading someone else's poetry or viewing another's artistic endeavors is different from what the student gains by creating such products for themselves.

Because of these highly varied perspectives, it is not surprising that there are many alternative conceptions of curriculum within the educational community. Furthermore, many individuals employ quite different conceptions of the curriculum depending upon the context. The same individual may view the curriculum in a quite different manner depending upon the content involved, the students involved, why the content is relevant to these particular students, and the preferred instructional approaches. In other words, how a given individual thinks about the curriculum varies greatly from one time and place to another.

These understandings of curriculum are important to us in our consideration of the role of religion and spirituality in the curriculum of the public schools. Religion and spirituality can be pursued for many different reasons and with a wide range of intended outcomes. Furthermore, this variability is influenced by the context. How such matters are pursued within the context of a pluralistic public education setting will be quite different from how they would be pursued within a more homogeneous faith community. Religious matters will be pursued in a different manner if the intent is to develop understanding of a particular religious outlook than if the intent is to foster certain elements of character derived from such beliefs. Particular conceptions of curriculum potentially have greater or lesser value to us for pursuing matters of religion and spirituality in the curriculum of the public schools. As a result, it is important for us to turn at this point to an exploration of alternative conceptions of curriculum.

Given the widely varied conceptions of the purposes of education—as well as varied understandings of such matters as the nature of learning—it is not surprising that there are many different characterizations of the curriculum. Curriculum theories are an active area of scholarship and the complexity of the field is significant. For our purposes, we will look at the curriculum from two different perspectives. One perspective, Schubert (1986), examines what he calls "images" or "characterizations" of the curriculum. He tends to center a lot on content, structure and activities. The other perspective, Eisner (1992), addresses alternative ideologies that underlie the curriculum. Both will be helpful as we consider the place of religion and spirituality in public schooling.

## Alternative Images of the Curriculum

The following set of categories for describing the curriculum are those of Schubert (1986). Although these conceptions of the curriculum vary substantially, they also have considerable overlap in that they often are intended to reach similar goals. On the other hand, the manner in which instruction would be pursued may lead to forms of education that are quite different from each other. Here is a brief summary of Schubert's eight images of the curriculum. After reviewing them we will turn our attention to their relative value in pursuing matters of religion and spirituality in the curriculum of the public schools.

### Curriculum as Content or Subject Matter

In this image, curriculum is equated with the subjects to be taught:

> Educators who use this image intend to explicate clearly the network of subjects taught, interpretations given to those subjects, prerequisite knowledge for studying certain subjects, and a rationale for the ways in which all subjects at a particular level of school fit together and provide what is needed at that level. (Schubert, 1986, p. 26)

### Curriculum as a Program of Planned Activities

The curriculum is viewed as a set of planned activities:

> The end of planning is to see that certain desired activities are delivered to students. Granted, all these plans have purposes for which the activities are vehicles. Yet it is the activity—what students do—that is the curriculum. (Schubert, 1986, p. 28)

### Curriculum as Intended Learning Outcomes

With a focus on ends rather than means, this image of the curriculum focuses directly on intended learning outcomes. The outcomes are a way of specifying purposes. This characterization of the curriculum fits comfortably with the current growing use of standardized tests as a means of assessing the success of schooling.

### Curriculum as Cultural Reproduction

Perpetuation of the extant culture is at the center of this image of the curriculum:

> The curriculum is a reflection of the culture. The community, state, or nation takes the lead in identifying the skills, knowledge, and appreciations to be taught. (Schubert, 1986, p. 29)

Examples of parts of the culture that could be prominent in the curriculum are the dominant economic system, or patriotic events of history.

## Curriculum as Experience

A curriculum focused on student experiences has been advocated widely in the past century:

> This position holds that educational means and ends are inseparable parts of a single process: experience. To attend to one's experience reflectively and to strive continuously to anticipate and monitor the consequences of one's thought and action relative to the good that they bring is a continuously evolving curriculum. The teacher is a facilitator of personal growth, and the curriculum is the process of experiencing the sense of meaning and direction that ensues from teacher and student dialogue. (Schubert, 1986, p. 30)

This image of the curriculum, of course, is commonly associated with the writing of John Dewey.

## Curriculum as Discrete Tasks and Concepts

The curriculum also can be conceptualized as tasks and concepts of importance to the students:

> The curriculum is seen as a set of tasks to be mastered, and they are assumed to lead to a prespecified end. Usually that end has a specific behavioral interpretation such as learning a new task or performing an old one better. This approach derives from training programs in business, industry, and the military. (Schubert, 1986, p. 31)

## Curriculum as an Agenda for Social Reconstruction

This more radical view of the curriculum calls for students to be agents of change in society. Societal ends, as contrasted with personal development, get higher priority than in most other views:

> This view of curriculum holds that schools should provide an agenda of knowledge and values that guides students to improve society and the cultural institutions, beliefs, and activities that support it. (Schubert, 1986, p. 32)

## Curriculum as *Currere*

This view of the curriculum, as in the case of curriculum as experience, emphasizes personal growth:

> One of the most recent positions to emerge on the curriculum horizon is to emphasize the verb form of *curriculum*, namely *currere*.... [It] emphasizes the individual's own

> capacity to reconceptualize his or her autobiography.... [T]he individual seeks meaning amid the swirl of present events, moves historically into his or her own past to recover and reconstitute origins, and imagines and creates possible directions of his or her own future. [T]he curriculum becomes a reconceiving of one's perspective on life... [and] ...a social process whereby individuals come to greater understanding of themselves, others, and the world through mutual reconceptualization. The mutuality involves not only those who are in immediate proximity but occurs through the acquisition of extant knowledge and acquaintance with literary and artistic expression. The central focus, however, is autobiographical. The curriculum is the interpretation of lived experiences. (Schubert, 1986, p. 33)

It goes beyond transmitting the knowledge, skills, and values of a culture and addresses self-understanding. This characterization of the curriculum emerged in the 1970s (Pinar and Grumet, 1976) and has received some attention in the scholarly literature since. It has not, however, been a major presence in the realm of "real-world" curriculum development.

It probably is apparent from examining this description of curriculum as *currere* that it has particular merit in connection with matters of religion, spirituality, and a wide sweep of existential questions. Such matters are at the center of one's search for meaning, are closely tied to one's past experiences, are highly personal, and take quite varied forms from one person to another. Such matters are not addressed readily within mass education as practiced in our schools, and they demand a high degree of differentiation from one student to another. The mutuality involved extends beyond the formal school setting to include family members, the student's faith community (if there be such), and other significant people in his or her life. Clearly, this approach demands a high degree of student empowerment. The issues at hand demand that the student take a high degree of responsibility for learning and not simply be a compliant participant in a highly structured mass education process.

## Curriculum Ideologies

Before exploring the *currere* image of the curriculum in more detail, we will examine alternative ideologies that may underlie the curriculum. While not totally different from Schubert's perspective on the curriculum, a close look at ideologies gives new insights. Elliot Eisner (1992) has written a provocative chapter about the various "curriculum ideologies" that give direction to a school's curriculum. A curriculum ideology—or "value matrix" in Eisner's terms—in any given school is what gives direction to the curriculum and justifies the choices made:

> In some ways, curricular ideologies derive from what might be regarded as *Weltanschauungen*—worldviews. Although religious ideologies, as they are played out in

schooling, often provide the most visible forms of ideological influence, there are many important nonreligious ideologies that have long functioned in schooling. (p. 302)

Eisner notes that such ideologies present to the public a position that shows "some array of curricular options" grounded in beliefs about what is important in education, some of which are overt and obvious, others of which are more subtle and less apparent. He notes further that some of the less obvious ones are the most powerful; when an ideology becomes pervasive "it tends to become invisible."

He recognizes that no single ideology alone determines the nature of schooling, since what exists results from a political process involving many compromises. Nevertheless, various ideologies—"a set of beliefs about what should be taught, for what ends, and for what reasons"—are reflected in school practice. Understanding the more influential ideologies operating in contemporary education will be helpful to us in our exploration of the role of religion and spirituality in education. The influence of various ideologies is constantly in flux, and this influence ebbs and flows as different constituencies work to shape education to their desired ends. Thus, attention is directed here to the six major ideologies he finds in American education.

## Religious Orthodoxy

Eisner's examples of religious orthodoxy come largely from private schools such as those of Roman Catholics, Jews—including those of differing belief systems—and evangelical and fundamentalist Christians, but he extends the category to others such as Waldorf schools. The defining characteristic of this category is an adherence to a well-defined and fully accepted orthodoxy which is to be passed on to students in an unquestioning mode:

> the aim of an orthodoxy is to shape the views of others so that they match the views of those who have already discovered the truth contained in the orthodoxy. Orthodoxies are not essentially about doubts, but about certainties. Indeed, to become orthodox is to become a true believer. (p. 307)

Education of this sort is not about helping students deal with ambiguities, but about conveying certainties that can be the basis for all of life. Beginning from such an orthodoxy—including both the religious beliefs themselves and related beliefs about the nature of education—one can develop a compatible approach to educational practice.

It is well to note that not all religious people are committed to such beliefs about the nature of education, *and* not all people whose religious beliefs are orthodox—in the sense of the term as used here—think that public education

should be conducted in this manner. The notion that all people with strong religious convictions are committed to education of this nature is a stereotype that
subverts productive analysis. Nevertheless, for some religious people it is true,
as evidenced by many of the political moves on the part of fundamentalist
Christians to alter contemporary public education with respect to such topics as
evolution.

## Rational Humanism

As with all of the six categories of curriculum ideologies, this one has variations
within it. Versions originating in the Enlightenment that emphasized the scientific method as the central means of understanding are found along with mod-
ern-day versions that view scientific methods as only one resource for knowing:

> The cornerstone of rational humanism is a belief in the primacy of reason and in a hu-
> man's ability to make rational and defensible judgments about the goodness of things.
> As long as this cornerstone remains intact, relativism must be rejected as a basis for the
> selection of curriculum content. (Eisner, 1992, p. 310)

The most obvious examples of this outlook today are the *Paideia Proposal*, which
was initially promoted by Mortimer Adler (1982) in the 1980s, and the Great
Books program promulgated earlier in the century by Robert Maynard Hutchins
and Adler. With rare exceptions, these viewpoints exist today as ideals rather
than implemented school programs. Hirsch's (1987) *Cultural Literacy* and Cheney's (1987) *American Memory*, a publication of the National Endowment for the
Humanities, display *some* aspects of this ideology—but certainly not all of them.

   The rational humanism ideology calls for curriculum content that is the best
that has been written and created by humans over time. Thus, we see the advocacy of the Great Books program. The methodology of instruction is of equal
importance. In contrast to an approach that emphasizes rote memorization and
multiple-choice and short-answer tests, the emphasis here is on developing the
powers of reasoning. Students are expected to give reasons for their opinions
and find "evidence and counterarguments to the views being expressed" in the
classroom.

## Progressivism

This ideology has roots that go back into the nineteenth century and was
prominent in the educational literature of much of the 1900s. Never so prominent in actual practice as in the literature, it has nevertheless been an influential
ideology. While commonly associated with the writings of John Dewey, this
ideology has several streams, not all of which are displayed in Dewey. It is also
well to note that not everything done in Dewey's name has been an accurate

reflection of his vision, and not all of his critics have made the effort to truly understand his position. But Dewey is the obvious first place to turn to understand this curricular ideology.

Eisner sees two streams within progressivism—the personal and the political—while also recognizing the limits of such a distinction because he sees the personal and the political as intertwined. For Dewey *growth* is a key concept, biologically, intellectually, and culturally. And it occurs in the school environment as students address problems of increasing complexity and difficulty. Eisner emphasizes three aspects of Dewey's thought as they relate to a progressive educational ideology. First, the total life of the school is important to Dewey, not just the curriculum. The school itself should reflect democracy, and even though students certainly would not have parity with the teacher in developing the norms and procedures of the classroom, they would participate in meaningful and significant ways. The classroom would reflect what society ideally would become. Second, the curriculum would have several features, but most importantly it would be problem centered. The teacher would create an environment in which students would tackle problems, beginning with formulating them, devising means of getting vital information, getting solutions, and assessing results—a process exemplified by science. Third, the role and duties of the teacher are critical. Creating viable problem situations requires "starting where the child is." Teaching is an art and requires knowing each child as an individual; it is important to treat each child as a distinct personality.

Even in the days when progressivism was most visible, it was far from the dominant form of practice in American schools. It is present to an even lesser extent today, which should be obvious to anyone who is aware of the current strong social and political movement toward the same standards for all students—not individualized—the focus on didactic instruction rather than problem solving, and assessment by standardized tests.

## Critical Theory

While critical theorists generally have not formulated coherent proposals for educational programs that lay out goals, curriculum content, and pedagogical practices, they have developed thorough analyses of current educational practice. It is more a means of studying education—and society—as it is, than it is a vision for what schooling should be in operational terms:

> Critical theory is an approach to the study of schools and society that has as its main function the revelation of the tacit values that underlie the enterprise. (Eisner, 1992, p. 314)

While the methodology employed could in principle have many foci, the writing coming from this type of scholarly analysis has largely focused on problems of racism, sexism, and class exploitation. It also tends to be highly negative in its assessments of education and presents a picture of its problems more than its potentialities. It paints a picture of an educational system based on tacit values that are biased against certain races, women, and those considered to be of a lower social class:

> Critical theorists, almost always on the political left, are typically concerned with raising the consciousness of unsuspecting parents, students, and educators to the insidious and subtle ways in which an unequal and often unjust social order reproduces itself through the schools. (Eisner, 1992, p. 314)

While there may be an implied program for the schools within their writings, critical theorists have not developed very specific proposals for action, nor have they established schools that could be evaluated against their implied goals. Although sometimes portrayed as an approach to research, it is appropriate to consider critical theory as an educational ideology. The products of this academic work have received considerable attention, and their potential influence on educational practice is significant.

## Reconceptualism

The newest of the ideologies presented here—it gained visibility in the 1970s—has been labeled reconceptualism by its originators. It is a way of thinking about educational programs more than a program itself:

> Like the critical theorists, reconceptualists tend to believe that American schools—perhaps most schools in Western industrialized societies—have been excessively influenced by a means-ends mentality modeled after a world that does not exist. (Eisner, 1992, p.316–17)

They have great difficulty with an educational program that is directed toward attainment of specific, standardized goals that are the same for all students.

Personal experience is at the center of their vision of education. Students must have the opportunity to focus on their own experiences, reflect on them in the context of other facets of their education, and come to a personal understanding of themselves, how they understand life, and how they hope to move into the future. Teachers should focus on the individual student and "try to understand the nature of his or her experience." The student must engage in a personal process that is in many ways self-defined. The teacher is at most a facilitator of this process—certainly not the director of it.

The reconceptualists have not developed school programs based on this outlook, nor have they developed processes by which they would be developed. They have not moved ahead in developing the teaching approaches needed to make these personal approaches a reality, which is somewhat understandable given their reluctance about routinized procedures and very specific outcomes:

> Reconceptualism is partly an attitude and unless teachers have acquired a disposition congruent with it, no routinized prescriptions are likely to be effective. (Eisner, 1992, p. 317)

The current strong movement toward standards-based assessment, and all that the movement entails, runs counter to the reconceptualists' agenda, but nevertheless this ideology is an important viewpoint in considering the place of religion and spirituality in the schools.

## Cognitive Pluralism

Although it has ancient roots, this ideology has only emerged as a unified outlook in the latter part of the 1900s. Its focus is on (1) plurality of our forms of understanding, i.e., "our conception of the nature of knowledge," and (2) plurality in our understanding of intelligence itself. It is a marriage of philosophical views of the multiple nature of knowledge and views from cognitive science about multiple intelligences (Gardner, 1983). Eisner, himself one of the shapers of this viewpoint, is committed to a curriculum with content that is broad—a curriculum that includes the arts, multiple forms of literacy, and multiple symbol systems from the various areas of human understanding, such as mathematics and science. Curriculum theorists such as Eisner have

> emphasized the plurality of knowledge and the unique functions of different cognitive forms. These conceptions have, in turn, served as foundations for their views of what school programs should teach and what educational ends should be prized. (Eisner, 1992, p. 318)

Gardner's views on multiple intelligences have received wide attention in educational circles in recent years, and there are isolated examples of attempts to put them into practice in school settings, with the leading example being the Key School in Indianapolis. The cognitive pluralism ideology in its more complete form has not yet emerged as a broad movement that is shaping substantial numbers of schools. But, as in the case of several others in this list of curriculum ideologies, it is fighting upstream against the current flow of politically driven attempts at reforming education.

## Curriculum Ideologies and Religion

What do these various curriculum ideologies have to do with our consideration of the place of religion and spirituality in public education? The application is not direct, but this portrayal of curriculum ideologies gives us a conceptual framework that is useful for our exploration of the place of religion in education. To be useful we must recognize some important characteristics. First of all, these six ideologies do not constitute a set of distinct, non-overlapping categories. Each one may have considerable integrity of its own as an ideology, but when a particular ideology is examined in detail, it will be seen that a given characteristic may be held in common with one or more of the other ideologies and an additional characteristic is quite similar to a different ideology or ideologies. Not surprisingly, we can expect that each will attend to religion in some manner, but that its place will vary substantially across ideologies.

It should be clear by this point that all views of education are ideological. Value-free educational theories are not possible, even those based on scientific research. Many educational theories are based on the results of social science research, such as theories of learning or social participation. To think that these theories are value-free, however, is obviously naive.

In relating these curriculum ideologies to religion, it must be emphasized that the category labeled "religious orthodoxy" is not equivalent to religious education, even when conducted in private schools. Certainly there is religious education which is well understood from this perspective, but to equate them is a damaging stereotype and a seriously limiting misconception. There is other religious education which is not consistent with this ideology. Note also that there is nonreligious education that follows this ideology; education is pursued in a more or less dogmatic fashion with little provision for ambiguity. The examples Eisner used for this category were not limited to religious schools; he included Waldorf schools.

Unfortunately, this misconception is not uncommon in academic circles, but it probably is partially grounded in misconceptions about the nature of religion itself. In contrast to some stereotypes, religion can be a source of freedom, a basis for positive mental health, the foundation of positive relationships, and can result in (a point based in the results of empirical research) better physical health and longer life. Similarly, education that is religious in nature is not necessarily dogmatic in character.

We must move beyond the six curricular ideologies under consideration here to formulate a viable approach to religion and spirituality in public education. Religion and spirituality themselves are multifaceted, complex, and connected to adherents' lives in numerous ways. Education that takes into account this reality—as well as the realities of human existence—is not simple and cannot be addressed in simplistic ways. As a result, the educational goals that must be addressed are multifaceted and the approaches to addressing them can be expected to vary substantially as well. Consequently, there are potential insights to be drawn from a number of the ideologies in developing a coherent formulation of appropriate public education in the area of religion and spirituality.

## Schubert's and Eisner's Views Compared

Schubert and Eisner have given us two viewpoints on curriculum, both of which help us see the multiplicity of forms that education can take. There are places where the two listings have striking overlaps even though they build on differing foundations. One is Schubert's portrayal of curriculum as experience and Eisner's ideology of progressivism. A second one—and the one I wish to focus on here—is the overlap of *currere* in Schubert's list and reconceptualism in Eisner's. They are talking about essentially the same thing, even though the former is a characterization of the curriculum and the other is an underlying ideology for the curriculum. This point of overlap is of interest because of their potential for addressing our dilemma about religion and spirituality in the curriculum.

Because the dilemma identified in the previous chapter has so many facets and is interconnected with so many educational issues, however, our analysis must be done in a holistic manner. It must address the many potential purposes of education, alternative learning theories, various understandings of student potential—such as Gardner's multiple intelligences—and the nature of the curriculum, among others. This multifaceted analysis leads to the use of this particular characterization of the curriculum—curriculum as *currere*—and its underlying ideology—reconceptualism—as a means of resolving the dilemma.

Curriculum is more than a matter of coverage. Students must be assisted with making interconnections among the parts of curriculum content and with related issues. The research is clear: without assistance, students see relatively few of the connections and generally do not transfer their understandings from one realm to another. Providing an authentic and complete education is of great importance. Without attention to more than complete coverage—including helping students make interconnections and drawing attention to the many personal dimensions of a topic—the education students receive is not only limited and truncated; it ends up being distorted and the source of misconceptions.

An authentic education must in important senses be personal. Whether it is a matter of one's personal experience of music, the application of aspects of biology to one's particular personal health issues, or the personal insights gained from a piece of literature, there is an important personal dimension. This attention to the personal dimension, of course, does *not* mean that students should be indoctrinated in some particular personal interpretation of a piece of music or literature.

Survey data show that matters of religion and spirituality are important aspects of life for the great majority of people in the United States, including the students in our schools. And even for students who do not claim any allegiance to a religious perspective, their secular perspective is an answer to questions all people face concerning the nature of reality, the purpose (or purposelessness) of life, and what gives them meaning (Noddings, 1993). In other words, a student's worldview is highly relevant to his or her education. Unless education goes deep enough to bring such matters to the fore, it has failed.

The fact that public education generally does fail in this sense may be an indication of the challenges in making education what it should be. The failure to adequately address these matters generally is not due to real constitutional or legislative constraints; this failure is largely due to other factors, including misconceptions about legal constraints, narrow conceptions of the nature of education, and what Stephen L. Carter (1993) has called the general "culture of disbelief." The challenges are many and not easy to overcome.

The thesis of this book is that significant progress in resolving this dilemma is possible and the means of making this progress are available. While this dilemma will not be totally resolved, significant progress in many areas is possible, including some of the areas thought to be among the more difficult, namely religion and spirituality. Potentially, a strong public school system can provide for individual differences among students, including differences with respect to worldview, religion, and spirituality. It also can encourage reflection upon alternative perspectives and growth in understanding.

Many people see little hope of resolving this dilemma in the context of U.S. public schooling. In their view, schooling is public and religion is private; thus, education cannot really be complete in the sense described here. But much depends upon how one conceives of schooling and the nature of the curriculum. Education is more than transmitting knowledge to students; it is a process of active engagement by individual students that requires teacher facilitation. It is individual education, not simply mass education. Authentic education is not impersonal; it is a unique process for each individual, a process in which the individual's engagement with the subject matter is personal and connects with their basic values and beliefs. Ideally, this individual process occurs in the context of an educational community where very different individuals have some mutuality of experiences that result in quite varied outcomes. Thus, we must examine more closely the image of the curriculum as *currere* and how it can be used to address the dilemma at hand.

### *Currere* in Practice

The *currere* conception of curriculum—or reconceptualism in Eisner's language—is largely theoretical and has not been the basis for extensive curriculum development efforts in the schools. Furthermore, it is an approach that runs counter to a large portion of educational practice in the schools. Extensive efforts will be needed to work out in practice how this approach can address matters of religion and spirituality. This work must be done in specific real-world contexts by educational practitioners. Such work clearly is beyond the scope of what can be done in authoring a book such as this. It is hoped that this writing will encourage such practical curriculum development and specific efforts to reform educational practice.

The results of this book may help to further this development process. In subsequent chapters, attention will be turned to specific areas of the school curriculum where matters of religion and spirituality are particularly relevant. In these specific contexts, the theoretical *currere* approach will be developed in more detail. Before turning to these specific applications, however, in the next chapter we will address in a general sense the possible place of this conception of the curriculum in dealing with religion and spirituality.

# SIX

## *Students' Worldviews and Personal Spirituality*

A basic argument of this book has been that education should be complete—that it should draw upon all of the human intelligences, connect with all major components of human culture, and concern itself with all segments of society. Given the prominent influence of one's worldview in intellectual life, and the important influence of religion and spirituality in our culture and subcultures, a complete education is not possible without their inclusion. But in our pluralistic society, with its constitutional separation of church and state, this rather ordinary educational expectation faces a constraint of major proportions.

In previous chapters we have laid the groundwork for a direct discussion of this dilemma by delving into a broad discussion of the goals of education and the nature of human intelligence, learning and teaching, and the curriculum. Matters of worldview and personal spirituality were addressed in a somewhat tangential matter. Now we need to address directly student worldviews and spirituality within this broader context. Typically, helping students develop their worldview and personal spirituality is not a prominent goal of the school curriculum. But if these matters are as important as claimed here, should they not be explicitly designated curricular goals? The counterargument, of course, is that this arena is fraught with too many land mines and potential hazards, so we need to steer clear and accept as necessary the risk that the family and other societal agencies will not do what is needed to fill out this complete education.

Certainly there are such risks, but there are other risks if this goal is avoided. There is the risk of an incomplete education as mentioned, but there is also the risk of the public schools "teaching," or presenting as the preferred alternative, a secular worldview as the "correct" one and spirituality as nonexistent or insignificant. Because our culture has a strong tendency to place matters of religion and spirituality in the private realm and avoid addressing them in the public square, public discourse—including the discourse of public schools—is largely secular in orientation. Even though public opinion surveys and other evidence show the overwhelming commitment of the U.S populace to some form of religion and spirituality, public discourse tends to leave it out of the picture, as well described in Carter's *The Culture of Disbelief* (1993). There is a de facto hegemony of secularism in public discourse that is accepted by people in general—at least partially as a way to deal with our pluralistic situation—and often strongly promoted by that portion of our populace having a naturalistic worldview.

My argument is that the risks of not attending to the students' personal process of developing their worldview and personal spirituality far outweigh the risks of the alternative. A complete education is needed; students' wrestling with ultimate questions should be affirmed and their attention to matters of spirituality encouraged. All of this can be done without endorsing a particular path for their journey or encouraging either a secular or religious destination.

## Developing a Worldview

An education with any depth is shaped by—and in turn shapes—one's worldview. This worldview is so foundational and stable that it shapes one's overall education to a much larger extent than the educational process alters this worldview itself, at least in the short term. Nevertheless, the process does operate both ways, as it should. It is relatively uncommon, however, for this involvement of one's worldview to come to the fore in a manner that is explicitly identified. It tends to be in the background of one's consciousness, while at the same time profoundly influencing one's response to new information and the process of developing new understandings. Less commonly—and typically over a more extended period of time—this worldview is altered in the educational process.

An important beginning point for both teachers and students is to simply understand that they do operate from a particular worldview. An additional basic assertion on my part is that the educational process is enhanced by making worldview considerations explicit and bringing them to the forefront of the process. If the learner recognizes an apparent inconsistency between his or her worldview and new understandings that are emerging, the educational process is moved directly to a deeper and more profound level. Intellectually, the stakes are suddenly higher; the motivation for serious work is intensified. The potential for significant learning is increased. There is reason to get excited about the learning that may occur.

Operating at this deeper level puts increased demands on the teacher. He or she must recognize differences in worldviews among the students, and obviously should do so without stereotyping or marginalizing anyone. This need for depth of understanding applies to the teacher's self-understanding as well. Failure to understand one's own worldview—including its complexity and differences from alternatives—puts the teacher at risk of making poor judgments in the educational process. It is also important in understanding new information that will be presented to students and the form in which it will be presented. To what extent is the content to be presented a reflection of a particular worldview, and to what extent can it be said to be free of any particular worldview? Such understanding is important to the teacher as the facilitator of a learning process.

Specifically, how can schools and individual teachers approach education in this manner? Let's start our exploration of this question by looking at the approach of Warren Nord as presented in his book, *Religion and American Education: Rethinking a National Dilemma* (1995). His analysis of the dilemma faced by American education has a lot in common with that of Stephen Carter mentioned above, but he goes beyond identifying the dilemma to advocate specific approaches that could be taken in the schools. He begins with elementary school:

> In elementary school reading and social studies classes students should learn that religion has been, and continues to be, an important part of culture; textbooks and stories should not convey to children that they live in a world free of religion. Students should come to know something of religious pluralism and our constitutional commitment to religious liberty. They should begin to learn about the holidays, customs, basic beliefs, and histories of different religions. An elementary education should begin to develop students' religious literacy. (Nord, 1995, p. 386)

He goes on to address other levels of schooling, and at the final stage of secondary education argues for "requiring of all high school students a single introductory religion course as the minimally adequate (politically feasible) solution to our problem" (Nord, 1995, p. 387). He is clear about this being "minimally adequate"; in his view, the ideal would be better approximated by a sequence of three courses somewhat like the following.

### World Religions

This course would address the major world religions with attention to their "theology and doctrine, rituals and religious experience, moral teachings and practices," at a deeper level than is possible with history courses.

### Religion and Modernity

The focus here is the role of religion in the culture wars of the most recent centuries. "Students should acquire some sense of the causes and significance of the secularization of modern Western civilization (one of the two or three great themes of modern history)." His reasons apparently are not just to understand modern times, but to improve students' overall education. "They should acquire a measure of critical distance on the secular assumptions that shape the courses they take if they are to learn to think reasonably and responsibly—and avoid indoctrination."

## Moral Philosophy

This is his capstone course, one in which students can focus on understanding "the implications of secular *and* religious ideas and values for contemporary moral, political, and social debates about abortion, sexuality, sex roles, justice, the sanctity of life, war and peace, and a dozen other issues (and they should read the arguments of all the major contending parties in primary sources)."

In Nord's ideal world, this three-course sequence would be required of all students, but he recognizes that it probably is not realistic in our social and political context. His fallback minimum position is one required course that focuses on the central themes of the above sequence.

Nord's approach (in either its one- or three-course versions) would provide an excellent context in which to address the worldview considerations I am raising. Given the orientation to the curriculum I have been espousing, however, I wish students to personally engage these matters. What is their personal worldview, how is it changing or being expanded, and how do they relate it to their overall intellectual perspectives? I suspect that Nord would endorse these goals as well, but addressing the means of reaching them appears to be beyond the scope of his book. My personal curricular ideal (inspired somewhat by the *currere* orientation to the curriculum) demands a personal student engagement and autobiographical connection.

What does such an approach look like in practice? It means that content is not learned just for the sake of knowing the particular aspects of content, but to understand its connection, or lack thereof, to other content. It means connecting it to contemporary social issues and, most importantly, connecting it to one's personal understandings in other arenas. It means connecting it to one's personal experiences in an autobiographical sense, i.e., how does this content relate to my current experiences and where I have been in the past? It is about interconnections.

The range of potential instructional techniques is great, but in general they will be constructivist (as defined earlier), personal, and interactive. Examples (from a much larger collection) would include journaling (personal as well as dialogue journals pursued with other students), small group discussions and collaborations of many sorts, and personal student projects. There would be a high degree of student choice of the individual work they pursue and not just "cookie-cutter" assignments in which all students are engaged in the same task.

In all of this work, a high priority is to be given to understanding their personal worldview, how it differs from alternative worldviews, how their worldview has been influenced by new learnings, how their understandings of new learnings have been shaped by their worldview, how the methodologies of various academic disciplines relate to various worldviews, and how they individually are integrating—or holding in tension—the understandings they are acquiring from various disciplines. The expectation is that they will acquire a liberal education in the classic sense of that term and in no way be subject to any sort of indoctrination, secular or religious.

With these goals, and using instructional approaches such as those just mentioned, much is dependent upon the competencies of the teacher and his or her ability to develop an appropriate classroom climate—one that is open, nonthreatening, and supportive of diverse viewpoints. Given this limitation, and the personal nature of this portion of the curriculum, I would make an allowance that Nord makes, i.e., allowing student exemptions from portions of the instruction in those rare cases of student or family concerns about the appropriateness of the study. With a competent professional teacher, I would expect such instances to be rare.

## Attending to Spirituality

The outlook of Nord which we have been examining is quite academic in the traditional sense of that term. Another approach, that of Rachael Kessler in her book, *The Soul of Education* (2000), is much more personal. The subtitle of her book gives a big hint of this orientation: *Helping Students Find Connection, Compassion, and Character at School.* Her approach is not in conflict with that of Nord; it is different. It grows more out of the students' personal concerns and less out of a content-based curriculum. Her focus is their "experiences that nourish their spiritual development and *yet are not directly related to worldview or religious dogma*" (p. xiv). She is convinced we can foster students' spiritual development without violating the First Amendment. It is an approach that does not begin with particular curricular content in the usual sense of that term, but one that begins with the students' personal concerns: "what young people wonder about themselves, about each other, and about the universe itself" (p. xv). She is convinced that with care, it is possible to address student experiences that nurture their spiritual development but are not related directly to either religious dogma or worldview.

She organizes her approach around seven "gateways to the soul in education." The seven are not a hierarchy or developmental sequence that students go through in a particular order; they are a set of seven gateways to nourishing the "soul of students." They are as follows:

1. **The yearning for deep connection** describes a quality of relationship that is profoundly caring, is resonant with meaning, and involves feelings of belonging, or of being truly seen and known. Students may experience deep connection to themselves, to others, to nature, or to a higher power.

2. **The longing for silence and solitude,** often an ambivalent domain, is fraught with both fear and urgent need. As respite from the tyranny of "busyness" and noise, silence may be a realm of reflection, of calm or fertile chaos, an avenue of stillness and rest for some, prayer or contemplation for others.

3. **The search for meaning and purpose** concerns the exploration of big questions, such as "Why am I here?" "Does my life have a purpose? How do I find out what it is?" "What is life for?" "What is my destiny?" "What does my future hold?" and "Is there a God?"

4. **The hunger for joy and delight** can be satisfied through experiences of great simplicity, such as play, celebration, or gratitude. It also describes the exaltation students feel when encountering beauty, power, grace, brilliance, love, or the sheer joy of being alive.

5. **The creative drive,** perhaps the most familiar domain for nourishing the spirit in school, is part of all the gateways. Whether developing a new idea, a work of art, a scientific discovery, or an entirely new lens on life, students feel the awe and mystery of creating.

6. **The urge for transcendence** describes the desire for young people to go beyond their perceived limits. It includes not only the mystical realm, but experiences of the extraordinary in the arts, athletics, academics, or human relations. By naming and honoring this universal human need, educators can help students constructively channel this powerful urge.

7. **The need for initiation** deals with rites of passage for the young—guiding adolescents to become more conscious about the irrevocable transition from childhood to adulthood. Adults can give young people tools for dealing with all of life's transitions and farewells. Meeting this need for initiation often involves ceremonies with parents and faculty that welcome them into the community of adults. (p.17)

As is probably clear from the above passage, her approach does not begin with particular academic content, as does that of Nord; she begins with student questions, concerns, and experiences and encourages them to "process" them with their peers. The striking degree of difference in orientation between their two approaches becomes especially sharp when looking at the forms of teaching expertise required. The curriculum that Nord is proposing calls for rather standard and conventional teaching approaches and skills. The approach of Kessler is strikingly different in what it demands. It cannot be approached in a strictly academic mode. It is very personal and requires a classroom climate in which students feel very safe to express themselves in a deeply personal way. It is not a curriculum with certain content to be covered as much as it is a collection of personal issues to be explored. She is focused on social and emotional learning. It would not be possible to give a conventional "end-of-unit" test to see how students ranked in their attainment of the goals of the unit.

As noted earlier, while Kessler wants to deal with student experiences that nourish their spiritual development, she wants to avoid matters that are directly related to worldviews. She is convinced she needs to proceed in this manner to avoid violating the First Amendment. This is the place where the contrast between what Nord and Kessler are advocating becomes sharpest. One is quite academic and the other is very personal. They are not necessarily in conflict, but they are different.

But there is a dilemma here that may not be as easy to resolve as Kessler seems to imply. Her stance is that situations can be established in which students address matters of spirituality without becoming engaged in issues of worldview. As noted in an earlier chapter, she says that

> young people have experiences that nourish their spiritual development and *yet are not directly related to worldview or religious dogma.* We *can* honor the First Amendment without abandoning our children's spiritual development. (p. xiv)

The problem is that worldview and spirituality are linked for adolescents as much as they are for adults, often inextricably so. Yes, there are spiritual experiences that can be related and discussed without delving into worldviews, but for persons whose worldview is intimately intertwined with their spiritual experiences, what gets put on public display in the classroom may be only part of the picture. Even though the First Amendment does not prevent individual students from describing personal experiences and expressing viewpoints that have a religious flavor—as long as all students have equal freedom in that regard—the classroom context can never be as totally unbiased and free as we might idealize. While students in this open classroom climate may be free to express their personal convictions, under the political reality—if not constitutional constraints—of the classroom, the teacher does not have as much of this same freedom. The teacher is in somewhat of a de facto agnostic position as a result of his or her professional role. Obviously, there is a resultant influence on the classroom climate. None of this is to say that the attention to spirituality that Kessler wants is inappropriate or should not be fostered, but the separation of spirituality and worldview is not as easy as she implies, and to not recognize this situation can be problematic. Is it not likely that this situation—and the view expressed in the quote above—results in a climate where spiritual experiences that are unconnected to a religious worldview are favored and that a subtle message is sent to students that maybe it would be best if you disconnected your spirituality from your worldview? Even though the goal of the courses is to foster social and emotional learning, the issue remains.

This commentary is *not* a prelude to advocating that spirituality be left out of the curriculum. It is simply a caution about glossing over tensions and dilemmas. In my judgment it is important to pursue a form of education in which students are encouraged to integrate their understandings from different arenas to the extent possible. This integration should not be a "forced" integration, just as it should not be an approach that encourages compartmentalization. The goal is a complete and comprehensive education with attention to boundaries and integration in a natural but systemic manner.

These considerations are obviously prominent with regard to the third of her seven "gateways to the soul in education," i.e., the "search for meaning and purpose." The "big questions" she includes in her summary description of this category highlight the prominent place of worldview considerations:

> "Why am I here?" "Does my life have a purpose? How do I find out what it is?" "What is life for?" "What is my destiny?" "What does my future hold?" and "Is there a God?"

My point is simply that we cannot ask students to address such issues and in any way imply that their worldview or religious convictions are not central to these considerations.

In spite of the apparent bit of hesitancy about having students delve into their personal worldviews, as noted above, the examples Kessler provides of student dialogue in her classroom show a lot of student openness and expression of their personal religious perspectives. She gives examples of students expressing deep convictions and describing personal religious experiences (Christian, Buddhist, and others) in a classroom with a diverse collection of students. A crucial outcome is the apparent sense of affirmation and respect felt by students of all kinds (religious and nonreligious) in a classroom where they can reveal their true selves without threat and with a sense of support for who they are. Her educational practice truly honors and supports diversity across the board, not just in certain limited spheres.

For someone wondering what Kessler's approach looks like in practice, her book gives a good description, including abundant quotations of student statements made in the context of the classes she advocates. As already noted, these quotations include a number in which students make explicit and personal comments about their religious perspectives and experiences. She certainly does not exclude them nor does she want students to be uncomfortable about expressing them. Her goal is a climate of openness and freedom to express very personal matters.

Still, there is a limit to how far these matters can be pursued in the public school classroom, even though they are of central importance to students and they could use some assistance in the process of addressing the issues. This limit brings us to the interface between what is part of the public school curriculum and matters addressed in the family and the student's faith community, if there be such. This is a matter to which we will return at a later point.

## Commitment and Wagers

A third outlook may help us round out our examination of the place of religion and spirituality within a curriculum focused on giving students a complete education. James W. Fowler's classic book *Stages of Faith* (1981) is grounded in developmental psychology and is developed with attention to its connections to other developmental theories, including those of Jean Piaget, Lawrence Kohlberg, Daniel Levinson, and Erik H. Erikson. Fowler addresses faith as a "human universal." He asserts that, "Faith is not always religious in its content or context." Questions which characterize his focus include ones about what commands your time and energy, what "causes, dreams, goals, or institutions" you are "pouring out your life for," who or what groups share your "most sacred and private hopes for your life," and the "most compelling goals and purposes in your life." Such questions in Fowler's eyes are human universals:

> To ask these questions seriously of oneself or others does not necessarily mean to elicit answers about religious commitment or belief. (p. 4)

Understood in this manner, these issues of faith are very serious business. They deal with "how we make our life wagers."

In addition to asserting that faith and religion are not the same, Fowler makes further distinctions. He speaks of religions as "cumulative traditions" which are "various expressions of the faith of people in the past." He sees faith as "at once deeper and more personal than religion." Our faith has to do with our choices and commitments—how we decide to place our bets in the business of life.

Fowler also makes a distinction between faith and belief. Although faith is often treated today as synonymous with belief, he is persuaded that "the widespread modern identification of faith with *belief*" is a misconception that needs to be exposed. He notes that the word *belief* has evolved in meaning over the centuries. While in current usage belief is about holding certain ideas, in earlier times it had more of a flavor of commitment or trust. His basic point is that faith is not the same as our modern understanding of belief with its focus on concepts and propositions. Faith has more to do with "an alignment of the heart or will, a commitment of loyalty and trust."

Fowler has a theory of stages of faith, including six stages which are elaborated both in terms of content and what he calls structure, an aspect quite different from the content. Elaborating these stages is beyond the scope of this book and for our purposes is unnecessary. He correlates his stages with those of others such as Piaget and Kohlberg. The comparison to Kohlberg's stages of moral development is of interest because of the assumed connections between faith and morals, and in particular because of the difference between the strong cognitive focus of Kohlberg's stages and the more emotive and volitional character of Fowler's stages of faith.

This is the point at which it probably is well to connect our discussion of faith to our earlier consideration of worldviews. Worldviews have a lot to do with our modern understanding of belief, including our understanding of the nature of reality. Both individuals and cultures have worldviews. In an earlier chapter a couple of specific examples of worldviews—theism and naturalism—were presented with some detail about the nature of reality, any purpose to life, the nature of history, etc., in each. The question at hand is how each student's worldview—whether one of these two or some other one—should enter into the schooling process.

Fowler's perspective, in contrast to those of Nord and Kessler, was not presented as an aspect of public schooling but, nevertheless, it is related. As Fowler understands faith, it is related to worldview; thus, his agenda is connected to that of Nord. On the other hand, he sees faith as related to psychological development; thus, there is reason to relate it to the work of Kessler.

Upon seeing the connection between worldview and Fowler's understanding of faith, it is apparent that we are approaching the boundary between Fowler's perspective and that of Nord. As should be clear from the discussion above, *faith has more to do with one's commitments than one's worldview*, but the two, faith and worldview, are far from unrelated. Given our goal of a complete education, one would hope that students would be making personal connections between them. What Nord sees within his purview has more of the traditional, or cognitive, focus of schooling. To consider the matters Fowler has in mind with respect to stages of faith, we must consider matters often omitted from traditional schooling, i.e., matters of personal action, choices "out in the real world," and reflection on personal meaning and purpose in life. Such life choices are a proper part of the school curriculum, although *not* in the sense of "teaching" students to make particular choices when confronted with alternatives in some particular situation.

Fowler presented his description of the stages of faith in the developmental process without much consideration of the context of this development, e.g., in solitude, school, family, faith community, or the broader community. Yet, the public school setting is one in which matters of faith are considered in the context of character education, service learning, exploration of career choices, and related endeavors. Students' "life wagers" (whether understood in religious or nonreligious terms) are closely intertwined with their education, and if schooling is to approach the ideal of supporting an authentic and complete education, it cannot rule such matters off-limits.

Taken together, the three perspectives of Nord, Kessler, and Fowler are quite complementary. Their insights, taken together, give us an expanded and enriched picture of what a complete education should include. But education and schooling are not the same; we need to extend our discussion of education more fully into the context of schooling.

## Putting It into Practice

Just how should these matters of worldview, spirituality, and faith be addressed in a public school context? This is the central question addressed in this book. Here is an answer to this question, sketched out in broad strokes. More detail will appear within case studies in later chapters.

### 1. Address the questions

Concerns about the separation of church and state, as noted earlier, have been prominent among the reasons educators have appeared reluctant to deal with religion, spirituality, and faith. These concerns are not a proper reason for avoiding these topics. In fact, it is essential that schooling give them a prominent place if education is to be complete and authentic. Unfortunately, this perspective is not part of the culture of schools generally, and the first step is to "reculture" the schools to bring their culture in line with the Constitution, proper pedagogy, and the goals of a complete and authentic education. The questions must be addressed—not grudgingly, but with enthusiasm.

### 2. Respect religious answers

Religious answers to these questions must be given as much credence as nonreligious ones, and the spiritual dimensions of life must be given as much consideration as materialistic ones. Possibly a more basic matter is respecting student answers in general. The questions at hand are ones that often demand personal answers that vary from one student to another; they don't have a "correct" answer in the textbook. In addition to establishing that student answers are both legitimate and desired, teachers must themselves honor answers from all perspectives—and establish a classroom climate in which students honor all perspectives. This challenge is a major one for many teachers; often such a mode of educational practice has not been prominent in their student experiences, nor has their preservice or in-service education given it sufficient attention, especially in terms of practical experience. The depth of the challenge, however, does not diminish its importance.

## 3. Be student-centered

Education of this depth demands that it address student questions, not just encourage student answers to teacher questions. Paul Tillich said it well:

> The fatal pedagogical error is to throw answers, like stones, at the heads of those who have not yet asked the questions.

While this comment applies well to all aspects of education, it is especially a propos here. A focus on student questions is essential if we are to move beyond a strictly "academic" study of religious matters. The approach must be authentically student-centered with nonstandard assignments (i.e., student selected and defined) and great freedom in the manner of pursuing them, including student collaborations.

## 4. Support students' commitments

The matters at hand deal with some of students' most significant choices and commitments. Students need affirmation with respect to the importance of these decisions, the difficulty of some of them, their role in the students' maturation, and their appropriateness in the educational process. Such support of their engagement with these life wagers, of course, does not mean steering them toward particular options. Such direction would be inappropriate with respect to the great majority of the questions under consideration here. Encouraging the student to seek out assistance from other sources, however, could well be very appropriate.

## 5. Seek family participation

One of these other sources of assistance for students is their family. While recognizing that for many teens in particular, this depth of engagement with their parents may be difficult, it also must be recognized that parents and other family members are among the most important influences in their lives when the lines of communication are at all open. A second connection to families is more programmatic. Dialogue between school personnel and parents is of high importance and can be especially necessary and helpful if attempts are being made to alter the school norms with respect to the issues at hand.

### 6. Seek faith community and other involvements

Connections also should be fostered with faith communities and other community groups. As in the case of families, they can both be a direct resource for students and an influence on school programs. What has been written here up to this point seemingly has been directed at an audience of educators with the apparent presumption that families and other groups would enter the picture when encouraged by the educators to do so. But they probably should not wait to be invited. There is considerable public sentiment—as evidenced by the push for vouchers and charter schools—that the schools have not been as responsive as they should be to parental concerns. If the schools have failed to give religion and spirituality their due, it probably would be wise for the public to make itself heard through their school boards, school advisory groups, and informal connections with the schools. It would be far better, however, if at the same time the professional educators were moving in this same direction and encouraging the public's participation.

## Laying a Foundation for Others

What has been presented here thus far largely has been written as if the schools were to do the entire job of educating students in matters of religion and spirituality. While such a presumption is inappropriate for any area of schooling—education is broader than schooling—it is especially so with respect to this curricular area. For many reasons—probably obvious—the family, faith communities, and other groups have a significant role to play here. An important question is how they all will interface.

I have no expectation of a coordinated system of cooperation between the schools and other groups in this regard. It is unrealistic, and in addition there is little reason to expect that it would have significant payoff.

I also think it is important for the schools to recognize that even if they give major attention to religion and spirituality, it is impossible for them to do the entire job. Thus, it is important that whatever the schools do, it provides a suitable foundation for others—students, families, and various groups—to build upon. Education is never complete and much of it of necessity happens outside of the schools; thus, schools should proceed as if the job is not done and they should make their pedagogical and curricular choices on the assumption that what they do is preparation for further student work in other contexts, both immediate and future. Given the acceptance of this position, however, we are still left with questions about boundary lines and just what constitutes laying a foundation for others. These questions will appear again as we explore specific case studies in future chapters.

### Specific Case Studies

We must now get more specific within the various curricular areas. Our previous overview has described many varied aspects of education, including specific knowledge, alternative worldviews, spirituality in various dimensions of life, and faith commitments. Not surprisingly, these matters show up in very different ways in different areas of the school curriculum. We will explore examples through case studies of specific topics or issues across the curriculum, and in the process take an advocacy position regarding what should be done. Specific actions will be explained and promoted.

In standard curricular terms, religion and spirituality are found most prominently in history classes. Whether in the events of ancient history or in such contemporary topics as the U.S. civil rights movement, accurate and intellectually viable history demands significant attention to such matters. Religion and spirituality also figure prominently in philosophy, but it rarely has any significant allocation of space in the K-12 public education curriculum. These are the curricular areas with the most content of a religious or spiritual nature.

The proposals of Warren Nord described earlier in this chapter fall in the history and philosophy space. Although much of this content could be included within history courses, Nord argued on a number of bases for a designated place in the curriculum for religion. I like his proposal (both the one-course and three-course versions) but recognize that their implementation in the schools will happen slowly at best. With or without such courses in place, history courses must be taught with appropriate attention to religion. In either case, such instruction is a cornerstone for addressing religion and spirituality across the curriculum.

A second part of the picture is appropriate attention to matters of worldview wherever they impinge upon the curriculum. Most often they are assumed or ignored, but they need explicit attention. Assuming a commonly accepted worldview on the part of students, or simply ignoring the worldview aspects of a topic, is a signs of a superficial education. To argue for attention to these worldview matters is not just an argument for religion to get its due; it is an argument for academic depth and intellectual rigor. Very specific examples are the foundation for the case studies presented in subsequent chapters. The teaching of evolution in science classes is a prime case in point. The methodology of science assumes a naturalistic view, although the personal worldview of working scientists in a large percentage of cases is a theistic one. Why is this neither surprising nor schizophrenic? Are science and religion always at odds? The central questions are not just about what science has to say about evolution. They also include how one personally integrates understandings acquired from different arenas through varied methodologies. The broader philosophical issues always come to the fore whenever one probes deeply into understandings from specific fields and attempts to understand them in relationship to understandings from other fields. Major portions of the case studies are directed to issues of this nature.

The third and final aspect is that of personal search and exploration with respect to what was earlier labeled "life wagers." The school curriculum is not unrelated to student choices and life commitments. Within the traditional school curriculum, they are most prominent in students' study of literature. Students read literature for personal engagement, not just as an academic exercise or to be able to do literary analysis. These choices also show up in less academic parts of the school program, such as a character education program, a sex education class, or a school anti-bullying program. Individual students' engagement in such education is centrally related to their personal religious convictions and sense of spirituality. In the cases which follow, such matters will appear as well.

## The Curricular Foundation

Prior to beginning any of the case studies, we need to return briefly to our discussion of alternative characterizations of the curriculum. Although matters of religion and spirituality can be addressed within any of the curricular orientations developed in the previous chapter, I am convinced that the *currere* characterization has especially strong potential for this purpose. It is personal and asks students to reconceptualize their past and present experiences in an autobiographical manner. It asks for student engagement that is individualized and not constrained to a particular pattern. Students are empowered to make personal choices about the particular student work they will pursue. In the cases which follow, this orientation to the curriculum is assumed for some *portion* of a unit of study regardless of what orientation guides the remainder of the unit. It is the approach that is being advocated for giving religion and spirituality their due within the broader set of purposes which may guide the unit.

# SEVEN

# Case Study #1:
## The Teaching of Evolution

No issue better characterizes the potential for conflict over religion in public education than the ongoing controversy over the teaching of evolution in science courses—a controversy which has continued in a persistent and tenacious manner for many decades. Over the decades, the controversy has taken different forms and the political battles have shifted from one setting to another—shifting back and forth at various times between state legislatures, local and state school boards, the courts, and the media, among others. The nature of the battle has varied as well, with opponents of evolution at various times promoting the teaching of "scientific creationism," the limitations of evolution and "intelligent design" as part of the public school science curriculum.

The ongoing public controversy and debate in many ways misses the most fundamental issues and fails to address questions central to any discussion of the goals of education and how science teaching can meet expected standards. For me, the issue is not whether evolution should be taught as part of biology, geology, and astronomy. Evolution is an integral and fundamental construct of these sciences and thus must be taught if authentic science is to be taught. Making this assertion, of course, does nothing to diminish the controversy surrounding the teaching of evolution. There is some hope, however, that the debate could be more enlightening—and that public education could be improved—by clarifying the central issues, identifying related curricular matters, and analyzing specific proposals for curricular and instructional change. Furthermore, there are specific actions which could improve educational practice in this regard.

Most of the controversy over the decades has seemed to be about which specific aspects of evolution—or some proposed "creationist" alternative—would be taught, and most often the underlying worldview issues do not come to the fore. But in my view, much of the controversy fundamentally is about which worldviews are being taught, promoted, or favored. Until these worldview issues are brought out in the open and their role in the conflict clarified, we will never have a good grasp of the issues.

## Premises

The analysis of the controversy that will be presented here is based on the following premises:

1. Formal education should give a central place to understandings we have acquired through the academic disciplines. While concerns have been expressed in earlier chapters about the compartmentalization of knowledge, these concerns were *not* about the value of scholarship in these various fields per se, but concerns about the compartmentalization of this scholarship and the failure of scholars to give adequate attention to the interrelationships of this knowledge.

2. A quality education demands that the nature of the subject matter, e.g., the nature of science, be addressed throughout. To be discipline-based means more than simply having a curriculum based on the knowledge attributed to the discipline. A high-priority goal of science education is for students to understand the processes by which data is acquired, conclusions are drawn, experiments are repeated, and other aspects of the scientific enterprise are pursued.

3. Authentic science education for a given student must be comprehensive, i.e., it must include attention to the full sweep of areas of human understanding—including the arts and ethics—and how they relate to scientific ways of knowing. It is important for students to understand the differences between scientific approaches to understanding and other ways of knowing. Science teachers have an important role to play in giving students this broad education.

4. Formal education must be done in a manner that enables individual students to incorporate these discipline-based understandings into their personal understanding of their lives in their totality. Students will not make many of the desired interconnections without assistance. Whether it is a matter of applying science knowledge to societal issues, addressing personal health matters from a basis of science knowledge, or exploring scientific ways of knowing in relationship to one's worldview, students need to address the interrelationships of their understandings from different arenas.

5. Effective education requires strong individual student influence over the process, i.e., understandings cannot simply be transmitted to students;

learners must be personally responsible for the development of under-standings. The comprehensive education sought here is not possible without students taking responsibility for creating personal understandings.

When looking at education in the broadest sense, these premises probably are not particularly controversial, but when the discussion is narrowed to that education which is a part of formal schooling, there is more possibility of de-bate. Much depends upon one's purposes for education and one's understand-ing of the nature of the curriculum.

An analysis of the ongoing controversy over the teaching of evolution must attend to the theoretical underpinnings of a wide sweep of educational dimen-sions—including educational goals, the nature of the curriculum, theories of learning, and current efforts to reform U.S. education. The analysis must be carried down to the personal level of the individual student. Thus, the analysis developed in detail in earlier chapters is central to the discussion which follows.

## An Approach to Teaching Evolution

A specific approach to the teaching of evolution in public K-12 schools is ad-vocated here. It is broad in nature and gives serious attention to student con-structions of their understandings. It has three key facets:

1. The science curriculum should boldly include evolution, current understand-ings of the origin of species and their diversity, and explanations of ongoing research in this area.

2. Care should be exercised in presenting models of the universe and the ori-gins of life so that their connection to particular worldviews is understood and both philosophical issues and the nature of science are portrayed accu-rately as a context for understanding.

3. Education should extend beyond the usual compartmentalization and spe-cialization of the academic world and challenge students to learn to think systemically and holistically and to integrate their understandings across con-ventional boundaries between academic fields and beyond them to other means of human understanding.

Each of these three points deserves to be developed a bit more completely.

## Boldly Teach Evolution

The first point above is unlikely to cause controversy in professional circles, even though it can be expected to generate opposition among some portion of the general populace. There is the potential, however, that full application of the second and third facets will lessen this public opposition.

Evolutionary biology is an exciting area of study, with new discoveries emerging often, and it has its share of scientific controversies—not to be confused with the acrimonious public debate over "creation and evolution." In other words, it is an excellent context for teaching students about the nature of science. The excellent resource published by the National Research Council (1998) titled *Teaching about Evolution and the Nature of Science* is an example of the resources available to help science teachers in this regard. Not only is the topic important in its own right, it is an excellent vehicle for pursuing one of the most important goals of science teaching—student understanding of the nature of science.

## Attend to Worldviews

While some opposition to the second facet may emerge in some professional quarters, it is argued here that it is absolutely essential for academic integrity. Words such as *theory* and *law* must be used accurately. The role of theory in scientific investigation must be understood. An understanding of alternative worldviews, e.g., a theistic worldview or a naturalistic view, is essential to understanding how different scientists locate their scientific understandings within their total understanding of "reality." These views vary widely among practicing scientists, as is indicated by one simple piece of data. According to survey data, approximately 40 percent of "working physicists and biologists hold strong spiritual beliefs" (Easterbrook, 1997, p. 890), a percentage that has remained essentially constant for decades. This data, and similar data from other surveys, are a strong indicator of the existence of a theistic worldview among a substantial percentage of scientists.

Obviously, many scientists hold to a strictly naturalistic worldview. No claim is being made here that scientists of these two persuasions necessarily approach their research in a different manner or that they necessarily have a different view of the nature of science. It is claimed, however, that their scientific understandings become part of a quite different mosaic of total personal understandings about the nature of "reality" and the meaning—or lack of meaning—of human life. None of what is advocated here for inclusion in the school instructional program differs from what could be found in the philosophy or religious studies courses of any secular university. It also is compatible with the ideas promoted in the previously mentioned National Research

Council publication, *Teaching about Evolution and the Nature of Science* (1998). Failure to give some attention to this second facet of the proposed approach to teaching evolution is to seriously truncate a student's education and probably also communicate an incomplete understanding of the nature of science.

## Personal Integration

The third facet of the proposed approach is more personal and more proactive in asserting the value of persons' attempting to integrate their understandings from the various realms of meaning to which they attach importance. It is not in any sense an advocacy of a particular integration of views. It goes beyond the second facet in not just saying that a variety of worldviews exist, but asserting that there is value in consciously examining one's views in various realms of meaning and coming to some integrated understanding of oneself and the world. The argument is that education lacking this orientation is narrow and incomplete. This is the point at which the *currere* characterization of the curriculum is especially helpful.

### Alternative Characterizations of the Curriculum

Given the widely varied conceptions of the purposes of education—as well as varied understandings of such matters as the nature of learning—it is not surprising that there are many different characterizations of the curriculum as developed in an earlier chapter. Our focus on the teaching of evolution requires that we refer back to these several images of the curriculum.

The three-pronged approach to teaching evolution presented above could fit within a variety of characterizations of the curriculum, including the curriculum as content or subject matter. The third facet of this approach to teaching evolution, however, probably would receive more attention in some images of the curriculum than others. I am arguing for serious attention to the third facet of this approach to teaching evolution. The argument could be made in the context of various curricular images, but here it will be addressed from the perspective of our preferred characterization, the *currere* image of the curriculum.

From the student's perspective, this orientation to education is personal, individual (though pursued in a social context), and constructivist. Within a social milieu, the individual student is testing new conceptions against personal constructions that grow out of a unique collection of experiences. It is autobiographical.

**Studying Evolution within a *Currere* Curriculum**

Is the curriculum limited only to the core subject matter within the various disciplines, or does it extend to the interface between disciplines, or does it go even further and recognize that there are areas of personal understanding that the thinking person must synthesize with the understandings they construct within disciplinary realms? The *currere* image of the curriculum clearly focuses on the latter. It is explicitly autobiographical and addresses self-understanding.

A major question for persons employing this image of the curriculum in formal schooling is how far teachers move from the content of the disciplines into the personal realm. Certainly, any constructivist understanding of learning is in some sense personal, but the extent to which the teacher is engaged with personal aspects of an individual student's life varies substantially between an image of the curriculum as subject matter, for example, and curriculum as *currere*. Some critics of the *currere* image have said that with this approach schooling would have to be conducted by a psychotherapist rather than a teacher. The vision of schooling proposed here, however, is focused more on the intellectual aspects of a student's life, although it does recognize that subject matter and the intellectual dimensions of life cannot be addressed adequately in isolation from emotional, aesthetic, or spiritual considerations. Such an isolated approach would clearly be a distortion of true education. The question that educators face, however, is how far they should go in helping students to address these questions and to what extent they leave this integration and synthesis up to the student alone. The question becomes even more important for public schools when one recognizes the relationship of this issue to religious considerations and the required separation of church and state—a matter that is accentuated in a highly pluralistic society.

In spite of these issues, education is not complete if it does not have this more comprehensive nature. Even if formal schooling is of necessity limited to some extent, it must be operated in a manner that takes into account the character of a complete education. Public education must be operated in a manner that takes into account, and *lays a foundation for*, steps the individual student must take, in addition to those explicit parts of formal schooling. It is my position that educators in public schools should go as far as possible in laying this foundation, while recognizing there is more to the job than they can do directly with the student. Students will get additional assistance from other agencies in society, e.g., a church for students so inclined, the family, and peers. A key question for public schools is what foundation they should be laying to help individual students grapple with such issues beyond the direct teaching of content commonly addressed directly by the schools.

**Examples of How the Issue Plays Out for Various Groups**

To provide a tangible example of the discussion at hand, a description will be provided of alternative positions that some individuals have taken with respect to evolution and its relationship to religious convictions. In providing this example, it should be noted up front that I am not proposing that this set of alternative positions be given a lot of time in the formal curriculum of the public schools as a set of alternatives from which students should select. It is presented here to illustrate some of the issues with which certain students are wrestling and to illustrate some of the positions which certain students may adopt personally in this area. It is of interest that, as of this date, a similar listing with even more descriptive information is included in the Web site of the National Center for Science Education, an organization devoted to the promotion of the teaching of evolution and opposed to the inclusion of "creation science" and related views in the science curriculum. They refer to their listing as interesting content for a lecture and as a reference point for discussing the nature of science. In other words, here is an organization with no interest in the teaching of religion in the schools that thinks this is appropriate content.

In presenting this set of alternatives as important background information for the teacher and as possible information to present to students, another disclaimer is in order; it is not a comprehensive set. This listing takes no account of positions that may be held by groups outside the Judeo-Christian tradition, for example, and there is no thought that the list is comprehensive even within this limited tradition. This listing of examples is diverse and certainly includes mutually exclusive positions—some of which any particular reader would reject emphatically. All of these positions, however, are ones held by a noticeable number of people in the United States. They are a part of the milieu of ideas that students encounter and which many of them are appraising and considering as a personal perspective. Each has been given a descriptive label along with limited explanatory information.

***Genesis as science.*** Commonly associated with people who would accept being called fundamentalist Christians, and often presented with a label such as "creation science," this is the position often reported in the media as being in conflict with the teaching of evolution in the schools. The bottom line for adherents of this position is that if there is an apparent conflict between the reports of modern science and their reading of the Bible, the Bible trumps the reports of scientists. On scientific matters, such as the origin of life, Genesis is viewed as a source of accurate information. Words such as *theory, law,* and *fact* carry very particular meanings, and typically little consideration is given to the role of theory in furthering scientific understandings. The position has a certain internal consistency but clearly is outside the mainstream of science.

**Intelligent design.**   Another perspective is that of people who are convinced that scientific evidence supports some evolutionary processes, but think that at intervening points, "intelligent design" was involved. Simple chance is rejected as the source of the particular patterns that have appeared in nature. While there is much debate about its potential as a scientific theory, it has some support from recognized scientists such as Michael Behe, author of *Darwin's Black Box*. While used by some people as a basis for attacking the teaching of evolution in the schools, it is of more interest here as a scientific and/or philosophical idea that some people use in their attempts to integrate their understandings from different realms.

**Theistic evolution.**   A common perspective among religious scientists, it is basically the idea that evolution has proceeded as described by science, but it was initiated by God. One variation within this broad camp might be labeled "Genesis as theology," since there are many biblical scholars who would argue that Genesis does not teach science but does have important theological knowledge. Some would note, for example, that this creation story was unique at its time for its conception of a monotheistic God who was outside of nature. The provocative question of the philosopher Heidegger may be appropriate for this category: "Why is there anything, rather than nothing at all?"

**Science as religion.**   For other people science encompasses and explains religion. It is a naturalistic worldview that says matter is all there is, religion is simply a product of culture, ethics are a product of culture as well, and history has no overarching purpose. Sometimes referred to as scientism, it also represents one of the fears of some religious people with respect to the teaching of evolution in schools. They are afraid that the teaching of evolution almost automatically becomes the teaching of scientism when evolution is taught with no acknowledgment of religion.

## Implications of a *Currere* Image of the Curriculum

The above examples of personal perspectives—though far from a complete listing—illustrate the breadth of ideas that a student with some religious convictions—a large majority of U.S. students—may be exploring in an effort to develop a coherent and integrated worldview. It actually pertains to nonreligious students as well, since essentially everyone at some point or another reflects on ultimate questions and the meaning of life.

The question at hand is: To what extent, and in what manner, ought formal schooling assist students in this personal exploration? Claiming the *currere* image of the curriculum as one's personal perspective provides a strong basis for aiding students in this personal exploration. But even given this commitment, the questions of "to what extent and in what manner" still are not answered. What does it mean to lay a foundation for this personal exploration?

### Putting a Personalized Approach into Practice

Our discussion of how a teacher can address the interface of evolutionary biology and geology with individual students' personal worldviews will be divided into two facets: (1) those aspects that can be taught by more conventional "whole-class" processes, and (2) those that demand more personalized and individual exploration. The former includes more academic study of the nature of science and matters of worldview; the latter includes the personal process of integrating one's many academic understandings into a consistent personal worldview.

### The Nature of Science and Worldviews

Teaching the nature of science is fundamental to teaching evolution, as is captured well in the title of the previously mentioned publication from the National Research Council (1998), *Teaching about Evolution and the Nature of Science*. Both evolution and the nature of science are treated as important instructional objectives and, for good reason, they are addressed in tandem. For decades, understanding the nature of science has been considered a fundamental and very important objective of school science. And the *National Science Education Standards* (1996), the widely accepted statement of current science education expectations, give this goal high status. This understanding of the nature of science is fundamental to understanding the nature of knowledge about evolution and the process by which it has been developed. They go well together because research into evolutionary phenomena illustrates the methodology of science, and an understanding of the means of scientific research, in turn, helps one understand evolution and the nature of knowledge in this area.

The previously mentioned book, *Teaching about Evolution and the Nature of Science*, provides many resources for public school science teachers. It is also well to take note of the approach advocated with regard to presenting information about creationism. On this question, the book is consistent with the *National Science Education Standards*, policy statements of the National Science Teachers Association and the National Biology Teachers Association, and definitive court cases, especially *McLean v. Arkansas Board of Education* in 1982. Teaching creationism, scientific-creationism, intelligent design, or any so-called alternative theories *as contending scientific explanations*, along with evolution, is off-limits on legal, educational, and scientific grounds. Fundamentally, the reason is that any search of the scientific literature will show no significant publication presence of research which gives credence to such alternative theories. While it could be argued that various forms of creationism have a significant place in the general culture and in various religious perspectives and thus would deserve a place in a class focused on religious studies, philosophy, or American culture, there is no basis for teaching them as a part of contemporary science. Thus, there is a sound basis for excluding such content from the science curriculum. While proponents of "intelligent design" often contend that their material deserves a place in the science curriculum as science, it has not passed the test at this point of having found a place in the peer-reviewed reports of scientific research.

The publication *Teaching about Evolution and the Nature of Science* is clear that many scientists believe in God and that many religious groups both believe in God and do not have a problem with evolution. Such facts are a partial basis for their stance that only science should be taught in science classes and that any religious material should be excluded. Science classes are to be a "religion-free" zone.

While fully agreeing on what should count as science, I am not convinced that this totally compartmentalized approach is intellectually or educationally sound. We need a more nuanced approach. And a more nuanced approach gives an opportunity to explore more deeply the difference between scientific, religious, and philosophical understandings. Their totally compartmentalized approach fosters narrow intellectual perspectives and provides cover for those individuals who, as part of the political battles over schooling and the general culture wars, are satisfied only with a hegemony of their particular worldview, often naturalism.

Truly educated persons understand their own personal worldview, how it differs from other worldviews, and how the understandings they have acquired from different fields of study relate to each other. This statement does not imply that we should expect our overall intellectual understanding of reality, our worldview, to have no inconsistencies or unexplained facets. While this situation should be our ideal—an intellectual goal—it would be naive to expect its total attainment. Nevertheless, it needs some attention during our explorations of knowledge within all fields of study; it should not be reserved for some special one-time course. Furthermore, few scientists or science teachers would want to convey the notion that science is important to the exclusion of aesthetics, ethics, and all other academic fields.

So, what does this broad intellectual perspective mean for how evolution and its relationship to various worldviews should be handled in science classes?

First of all, considerable care and effort are needed to help students understand the difference between the methodology of science, with its naturalistic operational assumptions, and naturalism as a worldview. They are far from being the same. A clear indication of this fact is, as noted before, the high percentage of working biologists and physicists that survey research indicates believe in a personal God and pray. In their scientific research, such scientists use data acquired through the senses and operate on the assumption that all of the data relevant to their investigation can be acquired in this manner.

On the other hand, they do not hold a worldview that says that all of reality can be understood in this manner. Almost all of them probably have some form of a theistic worldview in which God is thought to be personal, infinite, and sovereign; people are thought to have been created in the image of God with personality, morality, and creativity; God is perceived to communicate with people, ethics are thought to have their origin in the character of God; and history is seen to be linear with God's purpose fulfilled in people. Such a worldview is radically different from one in which matter is thought to be all that exists, personality is seen to be the result of chemical and physical processes, death is seen as the end of personality, history is a linear stream of cause-and-effect events with no overarching purpose, and ethics are said to have their origin only from people.

Two scientists, representative of two such worldviews, could pursue scientific research that would be indistinguishable in spite of their very different worldviews. This is not to say that their worldviews would never influence their work, for we know that science is not totally value-free and research is not totally independent of its practitioners' personalities. But in general, their work would be expected to be the same; they would be expected to employ similar methodologies, demand the same kind of evidence, and hold to similar standards—those of the scientific community.

The worldviews of the practitioners of science are far more divergent than the methodologies employed in their scientific practice. Frequently, scientists will be in agreement on the results of scientific research but then incorporate these findings into quite different ways of looking at the world, i.e., different worldviews. This understanding is fundamental to students' education and intellectual growth.

Second, it would be helpful for students to gain some notion of the range of means by which various people accommodate the results of scientific research and their particular personal worldviews. In my judgment, it is beyond the scope of a science teacher to present a full picture of such approaches and expect to help students make choices among them. For purposes of their understanding of the differences between the operation methodologies of science and worldviews, however, presentation of some illustrative examples is helpful and valuable.

A good source of such descriptions is the previously mentioned Web site of the National Center for Science Education, an organization founded to promote the teaching of evolution in the public schools. The director of the Center, Eugenie C. Scott, has compiled their eleven different positions under the heading, *The Creation/Evolution Continuum.* It includes paragraph or longer descriptions under headings such as Flat Earthers, Young-Earth Creationism, Progressive Creationism, Intelligent Design Creationists, Theistic Evolution, and Materialist Evolutionism. Her views on the utility of this continuum and its potential place in the classroom is apparent in portions of the concluding paragraph to her statement:

> Teachers of both high school and college have told me that many students come into a class with the attitude that evolution is somehow unacceptable for a religious person. Such students are reluctant to learn about evolution. One way to assuage their concerns is to use the "creation/evolution continuum" to illustrate the wide range of opinion within Christianity towards evolution, which helps religious students understand that there are many options available to them as people of faith. Most students will recognize themselves somewhere on the continuum, whether believers or nonbelievers; it makes for an engaging lecture. It is perfectly legal for teachers to describe religious views in a classroom; it is only unconstitutional for teachers to advocate religious ideas in the classroom. (p. 6)

It is well to note again that this statement comes from the leader of the leading activist group promoting the teaching of evolution in the public schools. I am persuaded that some information of this sort is essential in a science class where evolution is in the curriculum. At the same time, I would not expect to provide information in any real detail. Interested students need to pursue any options of personal interest on their own. Detailed explanations of how any one of these positions squares with current scientific knowledge is beyond the scope of the science curriculum of a public school. This is not to say that teachers should not encourage students to pursue such matters on their own, a topic to which we will return below.

A presentation of alternative positions such as Scott describes must be done with respect. It would be easy to disparage a position such as that of the flat-earthers with essentially no risk that a student in the class will take offense. But who decides where the line is to be drawn between what is to be put down and what is to be respected? More importantly, such respect creates a safe climate for students in which they can explore ideas and express viewpoints with low social risk.

Discussions of this nature can be an important beginning point for students in the important intellectual task of understanding their emerging worldview and how it relates to knowledge acquired from various academic disciplines. Acquiring such understandings is essential to students' intellectual development. It is part of laying a foundation for extending their education beyond formal schooling and connecting it to all parts of their lives—including the emotional and spiritual—and relating it to their interactions with family and other communities, including faith communities.

A common stance in professional science education circles is to avoid discussion of anything in science classes that is not science *per se,* i.e., anything that could be thought of as "nonscientific speculation." This stance has the apparent advantage of making clear what is and is not science and avoiding putting science teachers in a position of addressing topics on which they are not well prepared.

This stance also has many drawbacks. Intentionally or not, it encourages a compartmentalized view of knowledge and understanding. Unless explicitly addressed, this approach may imply for some students that science demands adherence to a naturalistic worldview, i.e., a nontheistic worldview, not just a commitment to a particular working methodology for science. This stance also may convey an image of scientists as people who are not interested in or committed to the importance of other arenas, such as the arts. It diminishes the importance of philosophy and other intellectual enterprises focused on the integration of understandings. It conveys a truncated and narrow vision of what education is all about. The controversy over the teaching of evolution should not cause professionals to retreat into a narrower conception of education.

If fear were replaced with courage, our vision of education possibly could be enhanced. Possibly we would be engaging students in discussion of differing meanings of the word "belief." Possibly it would defuse some—but certainly not all—controversy over the teaching of evolution because parents would have less concern about their children being "indoctrinated" with a naturalistic worldview. Possibly students would have a better understanding of the nature of science and how it differs from other ways of knowing. Possibly education would be more interesting and intellectually challenging.

I think the controversy over the teaching of evolution highlights the fact that our operating conceptions of schooling are limited, unimaginative, and routinized. Difficulties with teaching evolution in science classes is a problem in and of itself, but it also may be an indicator of how narrow and inadequate our conception of education is.

## An Aside about Intelligent Design

Through most of the last century, culture wars focused on evolution and creation have been prominent in the United States. These battles have taken various forms during different historical periods. During the last decade or so, the focus has been on "intelligent design," the self-chosen label of a number of individuals and groups who have been advocating an approach to science teaching with more of a role for a Creator in the origins of the universe and life. Because of its prominence in the current culture wars and political battles over educational policy, we need to digress a bit and discuss it in more detail.

The intelligent design movement is an interesting mix of intellectual currents and political and sociological phenomena. It includes a scholarly component of work, e.g., that of Dembski, which is intended to generate scholarly products that advance the intelligent design hypothesis. It also includes a strong political movement intended to sway public opinion toward a rejection both of biological evolution as commonly presented in elementary and secondary biology and earth science classes and of any naturalistic worldview. It is the conflating of these various facets that is problematic. They have been merged in the thinking and pronouncements of the movement and its leaders. Sorting them out would be helpful.

### The Serious Scholarly Work

Although most professional biologists and geologists probably dismiss the work of scholars such as Dembski and Behe as irrelevant and futile, it may deserve more respect. The physicist Paul Davies, for example, finds Dembski's philosophical and mathematical work to be a useful contribution to "mathematizing design," even though he also says he doesn't "exactly endorse Dembski's interpretation or his application of those design arguments to biology" (Giberson, 2002). Others have noted that less progress has been made by scholars in this arena than would be expected over the last few years, but nevertheless it is an area where capable people are pursuing a scholarly agenda that is relevant to important contemporary issues. Whether or not substantial progress is being made is somewhat beside the point. It deserves respect whether or not it is making a lot of progress.

### The Worldview Contributions

A valuable contribution of the intelligent design movement is its highlighting of the role of one's worldview in the evolution-creation debate, as for example, in the books of Philip Johnson. So much of the disputation in this arena ignores or glosses over the dominant importance of one's worldview, yet it is one's worldview that frames the issues and defines the terms of the debate. To teach anything about origins in the school curriculum without attending to worldview considerations is to shortchange the discussion and, in fact, usually seriously distorts the matter. As noted earlier, a theistic worldview and a naturalistic worldview, for example, are radically different in terms of any sense of purpose in history, the origins of ethics, or human nature. Any discussion of teaching evolution that fails to address matters of worldview is hopelessly truncated and inadequate. The writings of Johnson and others in the intelligent design movement have been useful in highlighting these issues and defining *some* terms of the debate.

## The Problematic Political and Social Agenda

While the intelligent design movement has made a number of valuable contributions to the discussion of origins and how worldviews should be attended to when the topic is addressed in public education, there is another facet of the movement that I judge to be seriously problematic. It is the attempt to significantly modify the teaching of evolution in the public school curriculum through a public campaign that largely poses the issue as that of conflicting worldviews. Furthermore, the campaign is conducted as an exercise in political power as promoted in a publication titled *The Wedge*, which has been circulated on the Internet and is said to be an older overview summary of material published in a book by Johnson (1997). It is somewhat ironic that many of the leaders of this campaign would decry postmodernism in contemporary culture, yet are proceeding in the postmodern mode of arguing almost exclusively from a personal viewpoint and proceeding in a political manner to sway public opinion, engage in political campaigning of various sorts, and change public education teaching on evolution through political activism among policymakers at the local, state, and national levels. The issue is seen as a prominent part of the "culture wars." The most problematic aspect of the campaign is that it defines the terms of the debate over public school teaching of evolution inappropriately, gets in the way of engaging the core issues of how to handle these matters in the public schools, misconstrues science, and encourages their opponents to take extreme positions as well. The result is polarization, gridlock, and wasted energy.

## Personalized Teaching

As should be apparent, I have been arguing for a different approach, one with academic integrity as described earlier. But there is a bit more to the story. I am arguing for encouraging students to take responsibility for more of their own education and extending their education beyond schooling to more personal engagement. That is the point to which we now turn.

I am advocating a curricular approach which emphasizes personal reflection and reconceptualizing one's autobiography, i.e., moving back into the past to reflect—in this case on one's worldview and its implications—and looking ahead to reflect on how one's view of reality possibly is changing and what the implications are for living life and planning for the future. Teachers should encourage this type of reflection and present it as the norm for positive living. It should be the expectation for an educated and emotionally healthy person.

Students should be encouraged to dialogue with other significant people in their lives about such matters. In most cases this dialogue is informal, although some family members and various groups may have it embedded in their family or group cultures in a way that actively fosters it. Schools should encourage this extended exploration.

It is appropriate for the schools to encourage such interaction through direct contact with families and groups such as faith communities. In the case of the specific curricular content under consideration here, evolution, this dialogue could be fostered by very specific discussion of the topic under consideration and explanation of which approach the school is taking. This communication could include information about the evolution/creation continuum presented above and an explanation of how the school is dealing with the topic, matters of worldview, and how students are encouraged to personally address these matters. Whatever the views of parents on the topic, it is important to treat their views with respect and encourage communication with them about the "collaboration" the schools are trying to foster.

Within the context of the classroom a number of approaches can be taken to encourage the student reflection endorsed above. An example of helpful student practices is journaling. Journaling and other personal writing can be a valuable process for students.

Various forms of dialogue among students can be valuable as well. An example is the use of dialogue journals. A student may journal about his or her means of relating their understanding of evolution and their worldview and then exchange this writing with another student who has an opportunity to write a response and give a personal reaction to the original writing. Obviously, this writing would be done from the outset with the understanding that it will be shared with a fellow student and that it is not writing which is to be turned into the teacher to be "graded." Dialogue journaling is a useful means of encouraging student reflection and expression.

Small groups can sometimes be used in a manner that is similar in function to dialogue journaling. This can take many forms, but an example may be helpful. In a situation where the teacher is aware of a number of students holding each of several positions on this issue, the students could be put in groups of students holding similar positions and given an opportunity to discuss their perspectives and possibly help each other clarify their understandings. As a next step, the students could be regrouped into "mixed" groups where they would have an opportunity to hear a much wider range of perspectives. As with the dialogue journals, no one is given a grade on the position they hold, but they are encouraged to engage in the important intellectual task of developing their worldview in dialogue with knowledge that is available from the academic disciplines.

Whatever student interaction takes place in the classroom, students should be encouraged to follow it up individually. While the number of students who do any such follow-up may be small, for those who do, it probably is a matter of considerable personal importance. In some cases this follow-up may be quite academic in nature. In other cases it may be more in the realm of the spiritual and their search for how they will make their "faith wagers."

## Making It Happen

Making this approach to teaching happen is highly dependent on individual teachers or, to some extent in larger schools, the collaborative engagement of teachers. While administrators would be expected to play a role in schools' deliberations over broader policies related to the role of religion and spirituality in the school, most often what happens with respect to a specific area of the curriculum will be dependent upon the teachers themselves, even in the case of something as volatile as the teaching of evolution. Thus, teacher education—either preservice or in-service—has the potential of being very influential in this instance.

How can one be assured that teachers are appropriately prepared to undertake this task? Information such as is found in this chapter should be part of initial teacher education classes, and ideally the prospective teachers would have an opportunity to student-teach in settings where these issues are handled appropriately as well. In-service education—especially when biology and/or earth science teachers are pursuing it with other such teachers—has similar potential. Ideally, it would occur in a context where the student teacher and the mentor teacher could develop teaching ideas together, have an opportunity to put them into practice in their own classes, and then evaluate the results in a collegial context. The potential for such education is greatest, of course, when these teachers have had a fairly broad and complete liberal education that did not promote compartmentalized thinking and was not constrained to certain worldviews.

It may seem that the teacher education just described would be sufficient, and such may be the case in terms of the more academic aspects of what has been advocated here. With respect to the *currere* image—or another transformational image—of the curriculum, however, the matter is not so simple. For a teacher to adopt such an approach to teaching, and do it well, is very demanding. For teachers who do not already teach in this manner, adopting such approaches is not simple. The demanding business of acquiring such abilities will be addressed in a later chapter. Similarly, establishing working relationships with parents and community groups, such as religious groups, is not easy to foster where it does not already exist. This, too, is a major undertaking.

## Realistically–Can It Be Done?

It could be argued that this proposal is problematic in that it places uncommon demands on teacher knowledge and competencies, arouses concerns about the presence of religious matters in public education, is too much for an already crowded curriculum, and gives education a personal character that is foreign to the current culture of schooling. Still others would simply argue that it is not the purpose of formal schooling. Whatever the concerns, it must be acknowledged that meeting this ideal of a complete and integrated education may be difficult within the constraints of our current educational system. On the other hand, it is a matter of the highest importance. Schooling should result in real education. In spite of constraints, teachers should make every effort to foster the complete education of their students.

# EIGHT
## *Case Study #2:*
## *Teaching Literature*

The focus of the previous chapter was a narrow topic, i.e., evolution, rather than the broad field in which it is found, namely the natural sciences. The chapter at hand is far from narrow. Even though it is not as broad as the language arts arena of which it is a part, it is nevertheless expansive and in many cases constitutes an entire course with a title such as American Literature or World Literature. Even so, we will focus somewhat. We are addressing reading literature rather than writing it. While literature is closely connected to art and music, we will limit ourselves here to literature per se. When literature and religion are addressed together, some may think of studying the Bible as literature or the Bible in literature. Neither gets our attention here. The intent is to address reading literature and the relationship of this activity to religion and spirituality.

It may be profitable to pursue a bit further the comparison of this topic with our treatment of the teaching of evolution. There are some important similarities and differences. An important similarity is that worldviews are a driving consideration. Whether studying literature from a detached "academic" standpoint or pursuing it from a personal, intimate perspective, worldviews enter the picture. All literary theories that can be used in analyzing a piece of literature reflect an underlying worldview, just as someone's personal grappling with a literary work engages his or her worldview. This interaction with worldviews pertains whether we are approaching it academically or personally.

Another similarity with our treatment of the teaching of evolution is our insistence that, if done appropriately, our study will become quite personal. Certainly, many educators would prefer to approach the study of literature in a more detached manner without really facing the personal choices that are brought to the fore, but a central contention of this book is that a complete and authentic education is not possible if done in such an impersonal and detached manner. Many of the issues raised in literature are truly personal ones—although the reader may not always recognize it—and if they are worth spending time on in schooling, they deserve to be made part of that education we are contending for—one that is personal, authentic, and complete.

There are important differences as well, one of which is the diversity of interpretive theories found in the study of literature. Certainly, there are different understandings of the nature of science, such as the differences between many sociologists of science and many established scientists themselves. But these differences are smaller than, for example, the difference between a literary theorist who understands literature on the basis of literary or aesthetic categories and one who sees the task as bringing out into the open the ideological and cultural perspectives of authors and showing their purposes and prejudices. The nature of science is a more unified topic for a science teacher than is the nature of literary theories for a literature teacher. One's choice among literary theories, of course, is not unrelated to one's worldview.

The goals of instruction are more diverse as well. Just as students are expected to study science so that they understand, in the same way, students are expected to study literature. But even though students are brought in contact with science for the pleasure and fascination it can engender, the role of pleasure is more prominent in the rationales typically given for studying literature; reading can be a decided pleasure. The difference between the two fields is much sharper when we consider matters of worldview. The arguments presented earlier for bringing worldview into the picture when discussing evolution are not common among most educators of science. On the other hand, matters of worldview are hard to keep out of the picture when one is seriously engaged with literature. In our consideration here of literature in the schools, alternative worldviews will be prominent.

A more obvious difference is that religion and existential questions in general are prominent in literature itself, while by definition they are largely excluded from the natural sciences. Certainly, the results of scientific investigations are relevant to individuals' consideration of religious and existential questions, but they are not the subject of research in the natural sciences. Because of this prominence of existential issues in literature, it is imperative that they be given corresponding attention in the study of literature as well. They need to be at the center of the study of much literature.

The selection of the specific part of the field to be studied is not as clear in literature and has been the subject of major debates in the field. What should constitute the canon has been a matter of great controversy. The culture wars have been intense, and there is no consensus even on what should be considered good literature. This diversity should be reflected in what students read, and they should acquire some understanding of the nature of the controversy about the canon as well.

Finally, personal choices and consideration of alternative viewpoints are a more obvious and routine part of the literature curriculum. Certainly, there has been some attempt to put consideration of societal issues and personal applications of science into the curriculum—not without controversy, of course—but their place is comparatively very small. Matters of personal spirituality and life wagers are at the heart of much literature and are a natural consideration in the literature curriculum.

These characteristics of the literature curriculum mean that literature teachers need to have a firm grasp of the full range of alternative literary theories, as well as the major worldviews found in our society that influence literary theories. This understanding is essential in an academic sense certainly, but it is also important in a personal sense. The teacher who hopes to do a good job in helping students wrestle with such matters must not only understand them academically, but must have an understanding of his or her personal resolution of issues—or an understanding of why they are not resolved—and what alternatives have been rejected in the process. The reflective life—a goal of our education—leads to people's knowing why particular choices have been made and what life wagers are being taken.

## Guidelines for Action

As noted in previous chapters, our major goals are twofold: to provide an education for students in a cognitive sense that includes the full range of intellectual ideas—in this case literary theories and alternative worldviews along with the relevant knowledge of specific literature—and to assist them in the process of addressing the spiritual aspects of life and the life wagers they are making. Three guidelines are presented here for the teacher who is setting out to do so.

## Selecting Literature

What literature should be selected to read in a literature class is a big issue; addressing it in any comprehensive sense is well beyond the scope of this chapter. The considerations that apply are numerous and all will not be addressed here. There are a couple of factors, however, which come to the fore when matters of religion and spirituality are addressed, and they will get our attention here.

Literature should be selected at least partially because of its consideration of existential questions. This statement may seem to be a truism, since it would be hard to find literature that we would think worthy of inclusion in the curriculum that did not address such questions. Nord and Haynes (1998) said it well:

> Virtually all "great" literature and art address and deepen our understanding of those existential questions about the meaning of life that are inescapable for any reflective

person: Who am I? What is the nature of humanity? How do I make sense of suffering and death? What is justice? What is my duty in life? For what can I hope? What is love? What is the human condition? Often these are called "religious" questions, in part because religions have traditionally provided widely accepted answers to them, in part because they are *ultimately important.* There are, of course, secular ways of thinking about these questions as well. Hence, we might say that literature and art address the central "existential" questions of life in *both* secular and religious ways (though sometimes this distinction is hard to draw). (pp. 124 – 25)

Given our social and political context, both religious and secular ways of thinking about such questions should be reflected in the literature selected—and favorable and respectful representations of both should be included.

Selecting literature partially for breadth of perspectives and worldviews is important but not always simple because of the many considerations that potentially come to bear. An example may be helpful. Gallagher and Lundin (1989) have discussed a movement in the latter part of the twentieth century to give a place in the canon to *Uncle Tom's Cabin.* Published in 1852, this novel depicts the horrors of slavery and its impact on family life and is an appeal for the abolition of slavery. It was the most popular American novel of that era and the first ever to sell over a million copies. In the more recent debate about its place in the canon, it has been considered by some to be sentimental and lacking in artistic quality. Others have differed, saying that though different in style from other novels of that era which are in the canon, it is nevertheless quite complex and artistic. Gallagher and Lundin then go on to raise a different but related point:

> Many modern critics see the world depicted in *Uncle Tom's Cabin* as "naive and unrealistic," since they believe only political and economic action can cause social change. Unable to grasp or accept the novel's premise that religious conversion can prompt social change, such critics deplore its narrative, characters, and language as naive, unrealistic and unconvincing. (pp. 108 – 9)

The point of this example is not about whether *Uncle Tom's Cabin* will make it into the canon, but about the *basis* on which decisions are made as to what literature students will read. Possibly this novel does not belong in the canon because its artistic level does not pass muster, but it should *not* be excluded because of a secular hegemony that excludes works written from a religious point of view. While a large percentage of present-day critics may not accept the notion that "religious conversion can prompt social change," this perspective is nevertheless a prevalent viewpoint among this country's populace, a majority of whom have a religious outlook. In summary, students should be reading literature that deals with existential questions, and this literature should approach these issues from a wide variety of perspectives and worldviews.

## Alternative Literary Theories

Literature is not just written from different perspectives—thus the selection issues above—it is read and evaluated from different perspectives. Again, we cannot be comprehensive in our consideration of literary theories, but some examples will help to show the diversity of perspectives. Although not very fashionable today, Romantic theories can be found:

> In Romantic theories about literature, it is commonly claimed that since science and technology have alienated us from nature and one another, only the imagination can make us whole again. (Gallagher and Lundin, p. xix)

Another perspective, religious in nature, is also described by Gallagher and Lundin:

> Though literature can provide us with relaxation and with images of the world as it might ideally be, it is neither an escape from reality nor a saving transformation of it. Instead, it enables us to respond to the order, beauty, and grace of God and his world and to the disorder that our sin has brought into the world. (p. xxiv)

Yet another perspective—one very prevalent in modern literature itself—sees a lot of meaninglessness in modern life and views literature from this perspective as well. This sense of meaninglessness often is an outgrowth of a loss of faith in God—at least a loss of faith that there is a God who created the universe, who reveals himself to people and redeems them. This illustrative list could go on, but a final—and quite different—one should suffice:

> several new critical theories suggest that literature is merely a big language game that readers play by interpreting stories to fit their own personalities and needs. (Gallagher and Lundin, p. 57)

Students should develop an awareness of alternative literary theories and bring them to bear on their reading of literature. How is one's reading of literature shaped by the literary theory employed? What insights are acquired as a result? How varied are one's understandings as a result of different literary theories? What insights about life, culture, and politics are gained as a result? Throughout their reading of literature, students should have the experience of applying different literary theories in a conscious manner.

## Student Engagement

While encouraging the application of different literary theories to their reading leads students toward personal engagement with literature and the issues it raises, it is possible for it to remain largely an "academic" exercise rather than one with a high level of personal reflection, consideration of personal insights, and application of insights to life choices. The more "academic" side, of course, is one facet of our two-pronged approach to a complete and authentic education. It is now necessary to attend to the second facet in our discussion of teaching literature—the more personal engagement with existential questions and matters of life decisions.

A transition between these two facets could well begin with the students identifying the questions faced by people in the literature itself, the manner in which they address the issues, and the resulting impact on their lives. The skilled teacher, of course, has many ways of doing so. From there it is a short step to having students consider similar issues in their own lives, in both the past and the present. A literature class is an ideal setting for education of this sort. Obviously, the potential of such an approach is highly dependent upon the class climate the teacher is able to establish.

## Putting the Ideal into Practice

Purves (1991) notes that reviewers of literature as a school subject see the subject, literature,

> through one of three main sets of lenses. One sees it primarily as a body of knowledge to be acquired; the second sees it as the vehicle for training in the skills of analysis and interpretation, and the third sees it as the vehicle for social and moral development. (p. 674)

A detailed assessment of the relative merits of these three outlooks is beyond the scope of this book, but it should be fairly obvious by this point that the third set of lenses is of particular interest in the present context. My contention is that even though all three outlooks have merit and a place in the curriculum, the third cannot be left out. To leave it out is to pull back from the full and complete education that has been advocated here. The emphasis among the three may vary considerably from one situation to another, but leaving out the third entirely is not a viable option.

Pursuing the study of literature at least partially for purposes of social and moral development means that matters of religion and spirituality are automatically part of the classroom scene. It also means careful consideration must be given to *how* the study of literature is done. Pursuing our ideal for the study of literature means giving thorough attention to classroom practice.

Here again the *currere* notion of the curriculum can be helpful. This image of the curriculum and the goal of social and moral development for the study of literature are a good marriage. An important focus is personal interpretation of literature and reflection on one's own life. The selection of the texts to be read is obviously a crucial issue—many would say the most important issue—but the manner in which they are approached in the classroom also is of central importance. It is the key to student engagement.

There are an abundance of teaching approaches that can foster this engagement, but whatever specific techniques are employed, the classroom climate is crucial. Students must feel safe in an intellectual and emotional sense. They should feel that their interpretations—even very personal ones—will be respected, honored, and encouraged. The previously mentioned book by Kessler (2000), *The Soul of Education*, is especially helpful in this regard. She provides excellent portrayals of what this kind of classroom looks like.

The specific techniques used for engaging students both orally and in writing are important, but a broad review of such approaches is beyond the scope of this book. There are many available resources for teachers regarding such teaching approaches, and only a few will be mentioned here as examples.

Giving students writing assignments in connection with reading literature which call for personal analysis and personal reactions yields different types of responses than assigned writing tasks that call for short answers or formal analysis. Research shows that a call for personal analysis yields interpretations that include more personal statements and are connected with students' other experiences. Some have feared that such requests for personal analysis would lead to "orgies of self-revelation" or would distract the students from the text itself. The research does *not* show this happening (Probst, 1991). With a positive classroom climate and a democratic mode of operation, there is every reason to expect that students can be so personal as to reflect and comment on religious and spiritual facets of their lives in a positive manner and move toward authenticity and wholeness in their education.

As mentioned in a previous chapter, journaling and dialogue journaling have substantial potential in the classroom. There probably is no place in the curriculum where these approaches have more merit than in the study of literature. Dialogue journaling where students share their writing with other individual students and receive written responses can be especially helpful to students in examining the religious and spiritual aspects of their lives and relating them to other facets of their intellectual and social life.

Harking back to our discussion in an earlier chapter of how learning occurs—and the importance of social discourse in this learning—reminds us of how valuable class discussion can be. Such discussion can be organized in many different ways, of course, and can occur in pairs, triads, and small groups as well as with the total class. For more personal sorts of discussions, the smaller groups have much to recommend them. There also are many opportunities to combine written and oral exchanges in ways that enhance the personal and autobiographical dimensions of the learning process. Whatever the details of the instructional process, the goal we are addressing is personal engagement with existential questions and the commitments of life.

Finally, it is well to note the potential for significant engagement of students with their families and faith communities in regard to these commitments and existential issues. For example, students can be encouraged to get reactions to their personal productions, e.g., written materials or dramatic productions. Another approach is to have students use families and faith communities as the source of ideas or perspectives to consider in the process of their engagement with issues raised in the literature they are studying. All can be important stimuli to the constructivist process of learning.

# NINE
## *Case Study #3:*
## *Teaching History*

A case study focused on the place of religion and spirituality in the teaching of history would appear to be one of the most straightforward and easiest of cases to consider. It most ways this is so, although all is not as simple as it may seem on the surface. No knowledgeable historian would deny the prominent role of religion throughout world history. It is also a straightforward case in the sense that history teaching with appropriate attention to religion is compatible with the traditional didactic teaching approaches that are so prevalent in the schools. This is not to say that this history teaching could not be improved by more innovative teaching approaches, but the desired curricular balance with respect to religion is not dependent upon having these innovative teaching approaches. The personal, autobiographical approaches advocated in this book are appropriate in teaching history as well, but are not essential for the desired curricular balance.

In addition to the simple matter of attending to the role of religion in historical events, three specific issues about the manner in which religion is treated are important for our consideration. Specifically, (1) religion must be addressed with sufficient depth—not treated so superficially that religion and its role are distorted, (2) secularization must be addressed appropriately, and (3) historical method and the role of alternative worldviews must be conveyed. These three considerations confront us and must be given adequate due if history teaching is to be what it should be.

### Consideration in Depth

In determining what aspects of a given topic actually are included in elementary and secondary school education, the best place to begin probably is with the textbooks that are used. Research gives strong indications that the topics taught in a given course usually are selected from the textbook(s) provided for the course and not added on. Textbooks typically include more than it is feasible for the teacher to cover—marketing considerations generally cause publishers to attempt to include all of the favorite topics of teachers—and teachers select from the book that which they think is most important. Since teachers have a tendency to think they need to "cover the material"—and the textbook is seen as a definition of the curriculum content—teachers generally select what they see as most important in the book and usually do not add much. Thus, if we want to know what is being taught in a given subject, looking at the textbooks is a good place to begin.

Based on his own analyses of textbooks, as well as analyses reported by others, Nord (1995) has reported a picture of what is included about religion in history textbooks. Although the situation seems to have improved a bit in recent years, the treatment is still inadequate. Religion actually is mentioned a good deal, but with respect to American history textbooks he examined, historian Timothy Smith (as quoted in Nord, 1995, p. 139) said they fall "far below the standard of American historical scholarship by ignoring or distorting the place of religion in American history. Where they do mention religious forces, the facts to which they allude are so incomplete or so warped that they deny students access to what the great majority of historical scholars think is true." Other investigators Nord cites conclude that religion is not treated as a significant part of American life, the American value system, or of importance to individuals. Nord says, "That the texts are inadequate is a matter of consensus," but notes that the nature of the inadequacies varies among analysts. He goes on to say:

> The closer we get to the modern West, the more religion disappears, and the few references for the years after 1800 are there for their political or social significance.... What is most obviously missing is any account of the intellectual, theological, or denominational development of religion after the Reformation. None of the texts say anything about higher criticism, the development of liberal theology, or (non-Islamic) fundamentalist responses to religious liberalism and modernity.... The secularization of the modern world, one of the great themes of modern history, is ignored.... None discuss the spiritual crisis of the modern world so much in evidence in the arts, as well as in religion (though one text does devote two paragraphs to religion as part of the modern "search for stability"). (Nord, 1995, pp. 140 – 41)

There is a long way to go before history teaching will include sufficient attention to religion, or this teaching is sufficiently in-depth. Better textbooks are clearly a great need, but there are forces that resist such changes. One reason is that religion is controversial in various ways, but another is that authors and publishers are secular enough that religion is seen as irrelevant, or lacking in a sufficiently truthful foundation, that religious dimensions are left out of the historical story. Teachers with sufficient depth of historical understanding are needed as well, and they have to be ready to bring this understanding into the classroom. The reasons for a failure of knowledgeable teachers to bring it into the classroom probably bear a resemblance to the reasons it is missing from textbooks—a fear of controversy and the general ethos of secularism that pervades the history-teaching community. A related phenomenon, secularization, is a prominent part of the history of the modern age and must be included in the curriculum itself.

## Secularization

Secularization—a major theme of modern history—needs major attention in history courses. But just what is secularization? According to Huston Smith (2001, p. 147), it is "the cultural process by which the area of the sacred is progressively diminished." Even though many individuals within a given part of society may be quite religious, public discourse tends to leave out this aspect of their lives, and the discourse proceeds based on the assumption that this dimension is not needed for effective communication. A systematic treatment of this phenomenon is beyond the scope of this discussion, but some of the relevant factors can be mentioned.

Certainly, the rise of modern science is an important factor. A seemingly unending number of natural phenomena that once were just thought of as "acts of God" now have scientific explanations, and an operating assumption of the natural sciences is that *all* such phenomena have a "natural" explanation.

This situation extends to the social sciences as well. Robert Bellah describes the assumptions of the social sciences as positivism (the methodologies of science are the avenue to valid knowledge), reductionism (explaining the complex from the simple), relativism (matters of religion and morality are not true or false but simply vary across individuals and cultures), and determinism (human actions are explainable in terms of the relevant variables). He goes on to describe how even though religion is a cultural phenomenon, it can have no underlying validity in view of these assumptions. Bellah, a respected social scientist himself, goes on to comment that

> Most social scientists would politely refuse to discuss the contrasts just mentioned. They would profess no ill will toward religion: they are simply unaware of the degree to which what they teach and write undermines all traditional thought and belief. Unlike an earlier generation of iconoclasts, they feel no mission to undermine "superstition." They would consider the questions raised above to be, simply, "outside my field," and would refer one to philosophers, humanists, or students of religion to discuss them. So fragmented is our intellectual life, even in the best universities, that such questions are apt never to be raised. That does not mean that they are not implicitly answered. (Bellah as quoted in Smith, 2001, p. 86)

Technology is a part of the picture as well. Human interaction and communication today among members of developed societies truly is global and not limited to one village. The power of technology is great and gives humans a control over their environment that was once unimaginable. Communication is now with a much more diverse collection of people with highly varied ideas of religion and non-religion; there is little local community consensus on matters of religion.

In this context, there is a tendency toward the privatization of matters of religion and faith—"the compartmentalization of religion that confines it to the 'personal' or nonpublic aspects of our lives" (Clapp, 2000, p. 195). It is a tendency promoted by the general cultural ethos—don't use religious reasons for a political position in the public square—and promoted by religious subcultures as well. There is, for example, an entire industry of "Christian music" with its own recording labels, large numbers of radio stations that play only this kind of music, and a separate category at the annual Grammy music awards—gospel music—even though most of the music is really not of the gospel music genre, but the category covers any of the music marketed to this subculture by this part of the music industry.

## Secularization vs. Secularism

In understanding the cultural phenomenon of *secularization*, we must distinguish it from *secularism*. Smith contrasts his definition of the *cultural process* of secularization as given above with his definition of secularism as a *point of view:* "*Secularism* denotes the reasoned stand that favors that drift (toward secularization). It argues on grounds that are cognitive, moral,. or both that the desacralizing of the world is a good thing." (Smith, 2001, p. 147). The methodologies of science are not only considered a valid way to knowledge, they are given an exclusive franchise. Any attempt to find first causes or ultimate ends is considered futile. It is the foundation of a worldview.

Understanding this distinction between secularization and secularism is foundational for students' understanding of the relationship between religion and other aspects of human understanding. The former is a cultural phenomenon; the latter is a worldview that is contending with various theistic worldviews. We are at the crux of a very important aspect of students' education: understanding the difference between various contending worldviews and their relationship to various fields of academic knowledge. It is crucial for addressing the fragmentation of intellectual life about which Bellah expressed concern. History is not just about political and economic events. It is about cultural changes over time—thus the attention to secularization—and about intellectual and artistic developments. Thus, secularism and its relationship to other worldviews demands attention as well.

## Historiography and Worldviews

What has just been said about intellectual life and various academic disciplines applies to understanding history itself and its character as an academic discipline. The work of historians involves the use of alternative interpretive frameworks. History is not just a matter of finding the facts and being sure they are right. It is a matter of interpreting the facts in view of all the information at hand. Not surprisingly, different historians have different interpretations and the worldview the historian brings to his or her work is an important element in this interpretive endeavor. The thorough historian gives careful consideration to his or her personal viewpoint and how it is influencing interpretations of the facts.

Are there competing interpretive frameworks the author might have used but did not? If so, what are they and why were they not used? Again, one would hope the historian has been open and informative about the matter.

The *reader* of history also must take into account personal viewpoints—in addition to those of the author—in interpreting history. Just what is the author's worldview—one would hope the author has made it clear—and how is mine, as the reader, similar or different?

These issues are particularly important when there are matters of religion and spirituality in the picture. If an event under consideration includes the religious experience of an individual or group, is it viewed from a secularist position with an assumption of no reality to it beyond the perceptions of the person or group? Or is the religious person's theistic perspective accepted as a plausible interpretation without prejudice?

These matters of interpretation are of central importance and deserve full consideration in the classroom. In a classroom with students committed to both secularism and various theistic (and other) worldviews, the discussion can be rich and deep and education enhanced.

## Curriculum as *Currere*

While what has been said here with respect to interpretation and worldviews pertains to conventional forms of instruction, it should be obvious that when the study of history gets to this stage, we are also reaching a point where the autobiographical approaches we have been considering are quite relevant as well.

How is history seen from different perspectives? This is not only an issue for historians; students must ask themselves what perspective they bring to their reading of history and how they see the relationship of this reading to their other understandings. Again, autobiographical approaches have considerable power. Many of the specific instructional strategies referred to in the chapter on teaching literature pertain here as well. Personal forms of writing, dialoguing with other students, and constructing understandings in a social context all have their place.

Scholars and students attempting to understand history from the perspective of a religious worldview are addressing a professional and/or personal endeavor that is challenging, exciting, and potentially very rewarding. Persons engaged in this task may have a lot to gain from the work of individuals attempting to understand history from feminist and ethnic perspectives. The work of people in these latter areas has been fruitful, and it is analogous in many ways to what the religious person is attempting to do. Communication across these boundaries can help to inform our collective and personal searches for understanding.

An example of scholarly work in this arena illustrates thinking that may occur in both the professional and the personal worlds. Marcus Borg, an American professor of religious studies (Oregon State University) and N. T. Wright, a British scholar, have coauthored a book titled *The Meaning of Jesus: Two Visions* (1999). Although both completed a doctorate under the direction of the same major professor (at different times) and both claim a Christian commitment, these friends have different ways of integrating their historical understanding into their overall worldview. In one case historical study of the beginnings of the Christian era is approached strictly by the norms of secular historical methods, and in the other case the historian's Christian worldview influences his historical interpretations. The book illustrates the influence of the historian's worldview on his scholarly work as well as the means by which a scholar integrates the findings of his scholarly work with his overall understandings of reality.

While the book is not one that a large percentage of high school students would choose to read, it exemplifies the sort of work to which such students may choose to turn in the process of fostering their intellectual and personal growth. It illustrates where personal and autobiographical approaches may lead in the process of a complete and authentic education.

# TEN

# *Case Study #4: Character Education*

Our previous three case studies dealt with quite standard academic parts of the school curriculum: science, literature, and history. The fourth and final one, character education, may well be the most challenging. But along with being complex and difficult, it may be the most informative to us in understanding the many issues pertaining to the place of religion and spirituality in public education. Character education seems to be something many people think is important—judging by its frequent mention in public discussion and the media—but there is no clear-cut consensus on what it should accomplish and especially on how to go about it.

Although the label, *character education*, would seem to indicate something more internal and mental, programs proposed for schools seem to be promoted on the basis of more specific behavioral outcomes. Some programs are focused on the prevention of violence and of bullying in the school setting, or of youth violence and teen crime more generally. Others are directed at more typical school goals such as increasing the graduation rate and avoiding dropouts. In some other instances the focus is on avoiding cheating in school and fostering academic integrity and interest. Others are aimed at reducing irresponsible sexual behavior and teen pregnancies. A bit different emphasis is reducing unmarried pregnancies and promoting two-parent families. The list could go on, but the point is that whether the list for a particular program is narrow or broad, character education programs in the public schools tend to be promoted on the grounds that there are desired behavioral outcomes, and the success of the programs typically is judged on the basis of such changes.

Character education can take many different forms. It typically is quite different in a public school context than it would be in the context of a church, synagogue, or mosque. In a public school setting it may be embedded in the ongoing events of the school, or it may be a stand-alone program that has its own spot in the program. This latter variation is a convenient distinction for our discussion of the topic since, among other reasons, it parallels the different orientations of two books that provide a good backdrop for our exploration of the topic.

## Operating Schools That Foster Good Character

Theodore R. Sizer and Nancy Faust Sizer have written a book titled *The Students Are Watching* (1999), in which they address the manner in which schools are operated and school life fostered. Their beginning point is not a designated component of the curriculum for character education but something that permeates the entire life of the school. They are concerned that schools be places that create an environment that convinces students that its teachers believe in them and thus are places where they can "learn well and deeply." It is this matter that is the beginning of our discussion of character education, because I am convinced it potentially is far more potent and influential than any special program that addresses character as a separate matter. Consideration of matters of character must be embedded in the manner in which the total school is operated, the way in which teachers relate to students, and the ethos of student life.

Good character is often approached as abstractions or principles to be used as the basis for a moral life. But coming to these matters as a matter of guidelines, rules, principles, or other abstractions does not have nearly the power in people's lives as does being in life situations where good character is lived out in the events of ordinary life. Furthermore, if educators are promoting certain ideas in the abstract but are directing the life of the school in a manner that is not consistent with these abstractions, there is little doubt as to which message is communicated most loudly. Thus, the beginning point for any discussion of character education needs to be consideration of the environment of the school and the nature of the relationships between people—both students and educators—in all their many manifestations.

Given the central focus of schools on teaching and learning, it may be well to begin with a consideration of the nature of teaching and learning as described in an earlier chapter. If the school claims to be pursuing goals of intellectual development, higher-order thinking, and the application of knowledge to personal and societal issues, the day-to-day practices of the classroom should reflect this pursuit. The role the students are expected to play and the nature of the work they are expected to do should be consistent with such goals. Furthermore, the nature of the relationships teachers establish with students and the expectations they set should be based on genuine caring and the best interests of the students, unimpeded by stereotypes and anything but the highest expectations. Relationships between teachers should reflect professionalism. Do teacher body language and tone of comments reflect negative judgments of other teachers or the respect and consideration due a fellow professional?

As a person who has spent a lot of time in dozens of different schools across the country in all kinds of communities, I know it is easy to come up with examples of instances where students are experiencing schooling in ways that do not meet these standards. But there also are the positive examples of caring and intellectually stimulating teachers, even though in larger schools with many bureaucratic procedures it sometimes seems as if they are hard to find. But the point is—aside from the proportion of good and bad examples—that the ethos of the classroom is critically important.

But it is more than the ethos of the classroom; it is the ethos of the school in its totality. What kind of collegiality and sense of collaboration and support exists among the teachers and between the teachers and the administration? What kind of "discipline policy" exists in the school and how is it implemented? Do students feel that discipline matters are handled fairly and that the persons in charge care about them? And, aside from the feelings of the student at a particular moment, was the action actually fair under the prevailing circumstances, and did the persons in charge really care deeply about the student? The answers to such questions depend heavily upon the school administrators, not just in terms of how they relate to students, but also in the manner in which they foster the desired ethos within the faculty.

Sizer and Sizer not only want institutions to model behaviors—and of course grapple with the questions of what to model—but to foster serious thinking about such issues with students. In other words, matters of value are not to be treated as simply extracurricular, but matters of moral concern are to be incorporated into the formal curriculum where they are subject to the intellectual rigor expected elsewhere in the curriculum.

In doing so, they insist that heed be given to both individual autonomy and the total school community. In seeking this desired balance, they give special importance to two words, the first of which is *voluntary*. The moral order must be established in a way that students do not end up feeling that the climate of their school is prison-like, as students will occasionally claim. They insist that the students and the educators partner in some manner both in creating the moral order and in maintaining it. While developing shared norms in small and voluntary communities can be done without a lot of formal rules, the task becomes more difficult in a larger formal organization. Coming to these shared norms in a school context is hard work, but worth the effort. It potentially results not just in the needed structure but in trust, a most important commodity in the school. Clearly, the adults in this setting have the greater power, but sharing some of this power in appropriate ways pays big dividends.

Their second important word is *equilibrium*. In addition to a unified culture in the school, there must be a place for expression of individual convictions in appropriate ways. While the two may at times seem to be in opposition, it is not necessarily so. One must be true to oneself as well as one's community. Finding the balance between the two is important for students to learn, and the moral order of the school should endorse and foster the process of finding this balance. Its importance may be especially relevant in the context of our topic here where expression of individual religious conviction is natural and necessary in a context where diversity prevails and tolerance becomes very important for the sake of community.

These thoughts bring us back to consideration of the topics of the previous three chapters, which focused on the formal curriculum in science, literature, and history. Sizer and Sizer see the central importance of these moral considerations in the formal curriculum:

> A central vehicle for this teaching is the school's formal curriculum. There are matters of deep value embedded in all sorts of traditional classes, in the sciences as well as the humanities and the arts.... Most teachers are fond of the word "engagement," because it means that the students are really taking an interest in the work which the teacher has designed for them. Grappling, however, goes one step further. It presumes that the student has something to add to the story. Either hypothetically or actually, the student is asked to join the struggle, to add his or her input. (Sizer and Sizer, p. 25)

Literature and history, which we just addressed in the previous chapters, are especially fruitful places for these considerations to take hold. The study of literature—"text-based" discussions—is a great place for grappling with these issues. It provides a valuable point of departure for deep thinking about ethical issues. History provides stories based in fact which also are excellent launching pads for moral discussions. Thus, our consideration of character education has brought us back to our deliberations about the place of religion in literature and history. If we are to have the desired equilibrium—i.e., where convictions embedded in individual autonomy have their rightful place alongside those of the community—discussions in classes such as literature and history must allow for—no, actively encourage—the expression of individual conviction.

Some people express doubts about the viability of this approach. Some doubt that all students are capable of this sort of intellectual grappling. Others see the increasingly prominent programs of high-stakes testing as a serious impediment to this sort of academic work. But an increasing number of people see that the moral is embedded in the intellectual and that grappling with these issues is both possible and necessary.

Finally, this discussion brings us to consideration of the meaning of absolutes—whether of religious or nonreligious origins. Some people on both the right and the left get concerned about attention to absolutes in the curriculum;

some fear that certain absolutes will be weakened; others fear certain ones will be strengthened. Sizer and Sizer are persuaded they need attention:

> The heart of it all, in school and beyond, is *thinking* about the practical meaning of absolutes. Such thinking does not necessarily weaken these absolutes. Rather, it deepens them. Civilized people are in the habit of thinking about the reasons for and the consequences of actions, and acting on the thought. (Sizer and Sizer, p. 118)

This thinking must be carried into the school context to consider the very operation of the school and the shared norms that are sought. It is the central aspect of character education in the public school context.

## Character-Forming Programs

A historically recent phenomenon in the public schools is the development of special school programs for forming good character in students. The intent of the programs is to shape character in ways that have visible outcomes in the behavioral terms defined at the beginning of this chapter. We need to examine closely what lies behind the development of these programs, the rationale for their inclusion in the schools, and what empirical research tells about their results.

Americans see much evidence of the fragmentation of their society and feel a desire for cohesiveness. They want a stronger sense of community, civility, and unity about the purposes and direction of American life. One result has been a desire for the schools to instill character in students, which has been pursued in numerous ways—including the introduction of formal character education programs. They are not unrelated to the moral considerations in the operation of the schools as discussed above, but they represent a quite different departure. They are formal programs to instill directly certain aspects of moral conduct in students, not just in the school context, but moral conduct throughout life.

A book by James Davison Hunter, *The Death of Character* (2000), is most helpful to us in this regard. Hunter, a distinguished sociologist at the University of Virginia, has tackled the topic of moral education in a comprehensive manner with careful attention to its underlying conceptual foundation, its various theoretical orientations, and its effectiveness in practice. Not surprisingly, as a sociologist he ties his analysis to the changing moral culture of our contemporary American society and probes deeply into its interrelationships with attempts to shape student behavior through school programs. His preface lays out a key claim which is developed in the book, namely that

> As it is currently institutionalized, moral education does just the opposite of what it intends. In its present forms, it *undermines* the capacity to form the convictions upon which character must be based if it is to exist at all. (p. xv)

A foundation for this claim is the results of empirical research that have been conducted on character education programs, of which there is a considerable variety. His conclusions from a review of this body of research about contemporary approaches to moral education are clear.

> The growing body of evidence, however, inspires neither confidence that the various programs are effective nor hope that modifying them will make them any more so. There is, of course, some variation in this. Some programs are better than others. But cumulatively, their effectiveness is at best less than impressive, and certainly not adequate to the challenge they are meant to address. (p. 151)

> The studies are myriad.... *In nuce*, these studies present conclusions that are as unambiguous and indisputable as any body of social scientific analysis can provide. The nub of it is this: *there is little or no association, causal or otherwise, between psychological well-being and moral conduct, and psychologically oriented moral education programs have little or no positive effect upon moral behavior, achievement, or anything else.* Even analysts who are sympathetic to this overall strategy have come to the same judgment.

> "The same applies to specific drug- or sex-education programs operating within this broad strategy." (p. 152)

Given the abundant effort devoted to the development of such programs and their implementation in a variety of school settings, the research results Hunter cites deserve our close attention.

He is not satisfied just to lay out the results of this empirical research but gives considerable attention to the underlying theoretical foundations of these programs and the manner in which they have changed over time under the influence of their critics. He notes that among academics and people developing these programs, a psychological orientation was pervasive and had no rival as a foundation for such programs. Traditional approaches to moral education were reinterpreted and religious ideals set aside. He notes that direct attacks on religious traditions were not prevalent, but they were "explained, rationalized and thus trivialized" (p. 70). By the time the underlying programs made their way into school practice, they were "overwhelmingly therapeutic and self-referencing." The programs had one central defining feature: their "center point is the autonomous self." He notes further that this orientation came to permeate all of the mainstream initiatives for moral education (p. 86). Of major importance in this emergence of an overwhelmingly dominant approach was the diffusion of these psychological viewpoints into the popular culture, which made possible the move of these programs into the schools.

The late 1980s and early 1990s brought a backlash against these programs, not so much in educational theory as in political rhetoric. While many of these loud voices were conservative celebrities, they also included traditionalists, feminists, classical liberals, and progressive humanists. The criticisms from these many quarters brought new approaches, which largely have been of two orientations which Hunter labels *neoclassical* and *communitarian*. He proceeds to analyze these new programs and says that he has to raise serious questions about any reformation. He concludes that

> The assumptions, vocabulary, and techniques of secular psychology are ubiquitous. Rather than provide a challenge and an alternative, the new character education simply reworks the psychological strategy within a traditional format of moral education. (p. 128)

Hunter sees little fundamental difference between the older programs and the newer ones promoted by the people of neoclassical and communitarian persuasion. But aside from this question of whether or not the newer programs are reformed, the basic point here is that all of these programs, new and old, are part of what the research says does not work. Current moral education is an utter failure.

## What Is Happening Here?

This analysis leaves us with many questions about why they do not work and what should be done instead. Hunter explores this topic in considerable detail and says that therapeutic individualism—the label he uses to describe the underlying theoretical foundation of these programs of moral education—is not just a pedagogy, but has become a worldview. It has permeated our common culture and become the operating basis of essentially all moral education programs, including those developed by the neoclassicists and communitarians. Hunter says that even though psychological moralism has "flattened out" the different moral cultures in our society, there still are clear differences in moral cultures and the consequences of these differences are important and quite discernible.

He finds abundant research data on the topic and notes that the common background factors social scientists typically use do not account for the differences in moral commitments. Factors such as race and ethnicity, age, gender, economic status, and family structure do not explain the differences:

> But against this one finds something quite remarkable: children's underlying attachments to a moral culture were the single most important and consistent factor in explaining the variation in their moral judgments. It was the children's rudimentary ethical systems, in other words, that provided the most far-reaching and dependable explanation for the decisions they made. These assumptions act very much like moral

compasses, providing the bearings by which they navigate the complex moral terrain of their lives. (p. 163)

The data generally show that the students who were "least likely to say they would cheat, lie, or steal, and the most likely to show restraint in sexual matters," were those with a theistic moral orientation in contrast to those elsewhere on a continuum which had expressivist and utilitarian on the other end.

### What Does Work?

This particular framing of the question of how to make character education programs successful implies a utilitarian basis for making a value judgment. But since the goals of such programs are so often expressed in such behavioral terms, it seems fair enough. Based on Hunter's work above, it seems clear that doing more of what is being done is not the answer. Since he also says—again, in behavioral terms—that students with a theistic moral compass have more of the desired behaviors, one might say that the obvious answer is to initiate moral education based on a theistic worldview. There are obvious problems with this approach in a public education context, of course, and we are back to a variation of the dilemma that keeps surfacing in this writing. Religion does matter. But within the context at hand, there obviously are many reasons why we cannot focus on it in the manner implied. We need a different approach.

It may seem that an answer lies in the idea of community. After all, the prevailing pedagogies are almost all asociological and if we moved to something more community-based, we might be able to make progress. Before jumping too quickly at this idea, however, it may be well to consider further some of Hunter's critique of current approaches:

> Grant them their due. The theorists of the psychological strategy do achieve their goal in theory if not in practice. The person envisioned by this moral cosmology is, in fact, autonomous—so much so as to exclude the possibility of commitments that go beyond subjective choices or obligations that are antecedent to personal choice. There simply is no framework for making sense of commitments that come, for example, by being raised as a member of a particular community or being part of a particular social stratum. If such constitutive attachments exist, they do so as an obstacle to moral development. So too, there is no possibility of a moral actor possessing, in a constitutive sense, moral perceptions that develop simply by virtue of having lived in a particular time and place in history. Likewise, any conception of good or evil bound up in the contours of an individual's or a group's identity in the constitutive sense is ruled out from the start. In this cosmology, the moral agent is alone, unconstrained, unencumbered, and radically self-governing. (p. 187)

Grounding moral education in community seems to have promise, but it is hard to envision any possibility that a community of the form implied by Hunter's critique could ever be established in a public school program. Morals have to be grounded in particularities—not just the self—and communities incorporating commitment to any such particularities within the public school setting are not feasible.

One may be inclined to argue—possibly vehemently—that such is not the case and community—inclusive of all students—can be established in the school setting which has grounding in particularities that all can accept. After all, the common school movement that Horace Mann promoted in the mid-1800s had this perspective. It must be recognized, however, that his approach was considerably narrower than would be possible today in that he was committed to a nonsectarian form of Protestantism, or possibly Unitarianism. Though broad for the times, it would be impossible today, not only for First Amendment reasons but because it would violate our norms of inclusion.

It may seem that a better case could be made by taking an example from a latter time period—specifically the approach advocated by John Dewey—but here again, the particularities are inadequate. With respect to Dewey, Hunter notes that

> underlying all is a working subordination of metaphysics to method—a subjection of some notion of moral reality, to which one must or ought to conform, to the process whereby morality is acquired. (p. 177 – 78)

By subordinating metaphysics, Dewey has in effect substituted a different metaphysics—one that eliminates many of the particularities that are so important for many students. Fraser (1999) notes that one of Dewey's many books was titled *Common Faith* and pursued the idea of a common faith that everyone could embrace as a foundation for moral education. He wanted to separate the religious impulse of people from any reliance on the supernatural. He was convinced such a move was necessary if any element of religion was to remain in education. The inevitable outcome of this approach is that the grounding of this religious impulse now is the self. And we are faced again with the problem underlying the current failed approaches to character education. Fraser also cites historians who noted Dewey's "blind spot" toward people with conservative religious views. While Dewey, with his strong emphasis on the social, probably would be unhappy with where some later psychologically oriented people have taken his progressive ideas, it is hard to see how any foundational commitment to the self in contemporary society's moral culture would not be grounded in therapeutic individualism.

Community so broadly defined as to include the entire cross-section of students in our diverse society has insufficient particularities to be the foundation for moral education. The problem is similar in the context of higher education.

Following upon considerable public criticism of the neglect of business schools to teach ethics and social responsibility to business students, a number of them have been given large gifts to initiate programs in this area. For example, the University of Denver received a gift of $11 million to establish a comprehensive program for teaching ethics to its business students, and the University of Colorado received a $35 million grant for the same purpose. But even though such institutions accepted the grants for this purpose, they now are struggling with just what kind of programs to establish and facing faculty concerns that such programs will have little effect (Griffin, 2002). The dilemma of how to approach ethics education is found at all levels, not just K-12.

## Adequate Community

Neither the self nor community defined so broadly as to include all of a diverse public school student body is an adequate foundation for moral education. If not, what then is an adequate approach to character education? It must be grounded in moral community, i.e., in communities which are defined by, and committed to living by, their moral stance. Of central importance are their particularities, i.e., the rituals and social networks that define their moral practices, the worldview that gives cohesion and significance, and the community story that gives them common understandings. Such communities are almost never anti-metaphysical. Moral education conducted in this context is not just a legitimation of American culture. Centering moral education in such communities is essential:

> Character outside of a lived community, the entanglements of complex social relationships, and their shared story, is impossible. (Hunter, p. 227)

These moral communities, of course, are not the school communities in which public education is conducted. They are families, faith communities, and other extant communities of people with a common story and a close network of relationships. It rarely is possible for the school to be this community.

## What Part Does the School Have?

If we accept the above description of where character education takes place—and must continue to take place—we are faced with the question of just what part the public schools have to play in this process of moral education.

## Operate a Moral School

The beginning point is the matter with which this chapter began—operating the entire school and all the classrooms within it in a manner that has integrity, is built on positive relationships between all—both students and adults—and is focused on education of the highest order for all students. Without this foundation nothing else will matter. With it there are other possibilities. As noted earlier, this goal is not a simple matter to attain. It takes a strong and sustained commitment and effort by everyone who is in a place of responsibility. It is at the core of any attempt to reform educational practice in a school, a topic to which we will return in a subsequent chapter.

## Give Other Communities Space

Acknowledge that most of the students' moral development is grounded in communities other than the school, encourage student attention to this fact, and make it publicly visible in discourse with students and the public. Our social fabric is fragmented enough that the diverse and wide-ranging moral communities of our society are not strong and vibrant by and large. Some may suggest that this fact means the schools need to take over and address this problem directly. But in the process the schools themselves become more fragmented as they attempt to do too much beyond their primary purpose. The schools would be better off themselves, and serve society more fully, by acknowledging that they cannot do it all—including formal moral education—and encourage moral education in the social context where it is obvious it actually belongs. The schools should view moral education as something done in partnership with these moral communities. How this process is to be worked out in practice is a major question. It deserves serious attention.

## Live the Diversity Ideal

We should revel in our diversity and celebrate its existence not just in such matters as ethnicity and gender, but also in terms of our membership in diverse moral communities. We seem to have a difficult time putting our diversity ideal into full practice:

> when it comes to the moral life, our educational philosophies and policies aggressively contradict the ideals and policies promoting diversity. We actually fear diversity of this deeply normative kind, and therefore do all in our power to domesticate the troubling particularities of moral commitment and community. (Hunter, p. 230)

Within our educational institutions we need to recognize our hang-ups, bring them out into the open, and diligently pursue this ideal. Again, we do not seem to know how to do this and we need to give serious attention to figuring out what it means and pursuing it seriously and with enthusiasm.

## Seek Commonality through Particularity

Part of the answer to living the diversity ideal is to find commonality through our particularities. The Enlightenment goal was to come up with an inclusive and universal moral language that everyone could accept. It not only has not worked, it has been counterproductive. We need to seek our agreements within our moral diversity and not try to pretend it does not exist and gloss over the reality of this diversity. This approach demands a new orientation to our life together as a public school community. It will require the courage to be open about our particularities, along with the sensitivity and compassion needed to accept each other in spite of them. Instead of culture wars we need dialogue and an honest desire to understand and accept each other in our diversity. It is a demanding task but one of the highest importance.

## Do Not Impose an Alternative Metaphysics

In the process of this dialoguing and seeking for community through diversity, there will be the continuing temptation to seek a common metaphysics and return to the Enlightenment solution to our problem. But to do so, of course, is to impose a different metaphysics on the many—actually it is a majority of people—who hold a metaphysics in strong conflict with it. It will undermine the process and needs to be avoided diligently.

# ELEVEN
## *The Role of Families and Faith Communities*

Education is not limited to what occurs in formal schooling; it extends to life outside the school. Within that broader world, a student's education generally is strongly influenced by his or her family, and in cases where the student is part of a faith community, it may have a strong influence on this education as well. Given the previously stated interest in attending to education in a broad sense—not just within formal public schooling—it is important that we direct attention to the education that occurs within the family and faith communities.

It also is important to recognize, of course, that the education that does occur in the context of formal schooling is substantially shaped by the context of the broader society. This shaping of the schooling process tends to reflect the more general influences of society, rather than the specific interests of a given family or faith community. Most families and faith communities have educational goals that extend beyond the more general goals that society as a whole has set for the education of youth. This interest is especially true in the case of religion and matters of social and moral development.

In this chapter we turn our attention to families and faith communities as they pertain to the education of their youth. In the process we will return to our concepts of completeness and authenticity in education and explore the sense in which such education, of necessity, extends beyond the boundaries of formal schooling. As a beginning point we will consider the education that occurs in faith communities, and in connection with such, in the family.

### Education in Faith Communities

Although education within faith communities is highly varied, some generalizations can be made. This education—formal and informal—is provided in the context of a community that shares religious experiences. That experience shapes—or at least has the strong potential of shaping—what one learns.

Individual experiences of prayer, relationship to God, purpose, and commitment are central to life in a faith community.

People within faith communities have made certain commitments, not just to the community but more basically to some religious understanding of their experiences and to living their lives according to certain principles and practices. Commitment results in new experiences, and these experiences in turn shape understandings developed in formal educational contexts, such as Sunday School classes, youth groups, and mission projects. Secular education tends to be provided in a context where objectivity and detachment are emphasized. To view a matter from a position to which one has already made a commitment is suspect from this perspective; detachment is encouraged. On the other hand, it restricts one's access to understandings that can only be developed from the "inside." Educational experience is given primacy within a faith community. Formal instruction within faith communities assumes some commonality of such experiences and builds from them and toward them.

Faith communities have shared understandings of experiences and their origins. Some are widely held across many religious groups, while others are limited to fewer people. For example, followers of Islam, Judaism, and Christianity—sometimes referred to as "people of the book" because of some common heritage—have some common understandings, e.g., God exists, God is personal, prayer is meaningful and important, and as a result life is different. For all of them history and tradition are important, and their scriptures have a central position and role. Critical-historical studies of these scriptures have a varied role across and within Islam, Judaism, and Christianity. But in all cases, adherents of these faiths are engaged in the hermeneutical process of understanding the implications of their scriptures for life in contemporary society.

Members of a given faith community generally are proceeding on the basis of a common set of assumptions, and the education provided within the community typically has aspects that are presented as givens without alternatives. Much of this approach, of course, is simply the nature of community. The community was formed of people with a common outlook; this commonality is what brought them together. As a result, education in this context can easily resemble that described under one of Eisner's six curriculum ideologies, namely religious orthodoxy. As noted earlier, in his presentation of this ideology, Eisner said,

> the aim of an orthodoxy is to shape the views of others so that they match the views of those who have already discovered the truth contained in the orthodoxy. Orthodoxies are not essentially about doubts, but about certainties. (p. 307)

All religious education is not that authoritarian, of course, but education provided within the community—for the purpose of furthering the community—
generally is not as open-ended as it may be within a public school context.

But all education conducted within religious communities is not so centered
on dogma. Some education is focused on growth of the individual and allows
for considerable interpretation. Even the study of scriptures can have this flavor. In Protestantism, for example, with its grounding in "the priesthood of all
believers," hermeneutics can be a process of discerning God's will for the individual, yielding a decision—made under the direction of the Holy Spirit—which
is not necessarily the same decision that would apply to any other person. And
it is not uncommon in such communities for the community itself to affirm for
an individual the appropriateness of certain actions in a particular circumstance,
or a unique "calling" to a special role in life. All religious education is not about
dogma, and in many faith communities their education fosters individuality and
freedom.

The perceived interface between religious and secular understandings also
varies greatly across faith communities. Continuing with Protestantism as an
example, we find highly differentiated outlooks. Three versions will be given as
illustrations. Among the most theologically conservative—including ones who
would accept the label of fundamentalist—are people who take the Bible in the
most literal manner. The creation account presented in Genesis, for instance, is
read as history and is not looked on as poetry in any sense. The universe was
created in six literal days. If there is a conflict between this reading of Genesis
and the conclusions of modern science, the Bible trumps science.

A second version—not uncommon among those who call themselves
"evangelicals"—takes the results of secular scholarship very seriously. Sometimes proceeding under the banner of "All truth is God's truth," there is a dili-
gent attempt to synthesize biblical understandings and those that prevail in the
secular academy. The hermeneutics employed in these circles recognize the cultural context in which the Bible was written, treat the biblical documents as reli-
able historical documents—while recognizing that these documents are quite
varied in literary form, including historical accounts, poetry, etc.—and seek to
understand their implications for faith and life today. The results of modern
scholarship are sought with enthusiasm while rejecting the atheistic worldview
sometimes associated with it.

The third perspective—one not uncommon among those who call themselves "liberal Protestants"—treats the Bible in yet another way. Critical-
historical methods dominate the study of the Bible, and if there is an apparent
conflict between a biblical account and modern scholarship—say in the Genesis
account of the origins of the universe and life—there is little perceived need to

reconcile them. Modern science has the answers. The basic doctrines of Christianity are affirmed but the historicity of events as recorded in the Bible is not a watershed matter. A theistic worldview and the validity of experiences found in the Christian tradition are foundations of this perspective.

A similar range of perspectives can be found in other parts of Christendom, within Judaism, and in other religious traditions. This range of perspectives also is indicative of the range of understandings of the nature of religious education. As noted earlier, the variation in educational ideologies that prevail within and across religious categories is substantial. This range undoubtedly prevails across families as well.

Given the principle of separation of church and state, public schools are not in a position to teach explicitly that any particular worldview (religious or secular) is the "correct" one. The range of contenders is given equitable treatment and under these circumstances, no specific worldview is likely to be taught to students in any detail. This situation provides an incentive for faith communities to give serious attention to providing such education from their perspective to their youth. Furthermore, given the secular nature of the general culture, and a perceived hegemony of secular perspectives in schools due to a hypersensitivity to possible violation of the principle of separation of church and state, faith communities have an additional incentive to take significant steps in this regard.

In actual fact, most faith communities probably do not expend great direct effort in education about worldview issues. Such matters probably enter the picture more indirectly in the context of activities focused on spiritual considerations and the faith commitments of their youth, but the time that faith communities have for education is quite limited. Faith communities should recognize, however, that if they want such education done, they will have to do a lot of it themselves. They can develop and conduct educational programs that engage the issues under discussion in this book in more depth from the perspective of their particular faith tradition. Given a good foundation in the public school context, such programs can both enhance the work of the schools and forge additional understandings from a different perspective. To achieve substantial progress in helping their youth develop more sophisticated worldview understandings, faith communities need to understand what schools are accomplishing and build on the foundation developed there. This need is an important reason for faith communities to have an open line of communication with the schools. Their goals are complementary.

## The Interface of Public Schooling and Other Education

In an earlier chapter considerable attention was given to the nature of a complete education. We need to bear it in mind as we consider how education in the context of formal schooling interfaces with the student's education in other contexts. Our ideal education gives attention to multiple intelligences (Gardner, 1999) and the multiplicity of goals they imply, alternative worldviews, means of bridging compartmentalized knowledge, the integration of knowledge, applications of knowledge to societal issues and personal life, and curricular balance. Furthermore, it is personal and provides student empowerment and individual choice.

Public schooling does not provide—and probably never can provide—a complete education in this sense. This situation is not just a result of strictures on religious content in the curriculum due to the separation of church and state. It is related to the compartmentalization of academic disciplines, extant public understanding of the goals of education, the impersonal nature of so many relationships in contemporary society, and cultural norms for student empowerment and choice. But even though a complete education is an impossible task for the public schools, it is a critically important goal that should be pursued to the fullest extent possible. Its pursuit should permeate the curriculum and push the schooling enterprise as close as possible to this ideal.

Given that much of education takes place outside the bounds of the public school, educators should make every attempt to connect what they are doing to other aspects of education within various informal settings and in students' lives in general. To do so, the public school teacher must know something of the students' lives outside the school context, understand the other forms of education that engage the students, and have communication with parents and others who are part of the education processes in which various students are engaged.

Such knowledge and interaction are not easy for a teacher to attain for many reasons—not the least of which is the time required and having the means of communication. Another reason is the diversity of educational ideologies within religious communities, which means that students come to public schools with quite diverse outlooks, teacher interactions with parents have a highly varied form as well, and communication is limited by parents' highly varied conceptions of what public school should be.

Nevertheless, family members and groups within the community have much to contribute to formal instruction regarding the role of religion in history or alternative worldviews. They can, in fact, be rich resources. It is not a matter of going to them to get the "right answers," but to get additional information, specific instances for reflection, and alternative outlooks. When it comes to matters of spirituality (Kessler, 2000) and making life choices, the anticipated benefits are even larger. Again, it is not a matter of student choices and commitments being determined by others, but having an opportunity to dialogue and gain insights available in a healthy family and/or community context. The richness of this personal interaction potentially goes far beyond what is typically available in a school context, given the reality of student-teacher ratios and overcrowded time schedules.

Students may or may not take the initiative in utilizing these potential resources. Their use should be encouraged by teachers, just as good teachers encourage the wide use of multiple resources throughout the curriculum. Good teachers tend to be imaginative in the type of student work they promote and the student roles they foster. Given the curricular goals advocated here, these same skilled teachers can be expected to promote innovative student work and encourage independent and productive student roles.

Similarly, wise and well-informed parents—as well as leaders in faith communities—will take the initiative in fostering the desired interaction by their direct involvement with these students, and possibly through communication with the teacher. Granted that in many instances parental involvement in formal schooling is quite limited, it is still important that education extend beyond formal schooling. Everyone involved should do their part in promoting such an authentic education—one that extends beyond formal schooling. Superior education demands student initiative in taking charge of their own learning. Everyone involved—teachers, parents, and youth leaders—should do their best to promote and support it.

## Parental Influence on Schooling

In addition to playing a direct role in helping an individual student extend his or her schooling into a complete education, parents can have an influence on the schooling itself. The political structure of American public education, our social arrangements, and our cultural expectations all lead to significant public influence on schooling. Formal processes such as the election of local school boards and participation on school advisory groups are routine. The demand for even greater influence over the education of their children has led to vouchers and charter schools in many states in the last couple of decades. These later developments reflect not only a high level of importance ascribed to schooling but a considerable level of distrust of the educational system in its traditional form. A considerable portion of the public perceives the public school system as intransigent and its leaders as resistant to change.

But this resistance to change goes in the opposite direction as well. In many places where schools have made substantial changes and attempted to improve education, they have met with resistance from parents. Seemingly there is always great resistance to major educational changes, regardless of the particular changes or who initiates them. The research on educational reform is extensive—as will be seen in the next chapter—and it documents this phenomenon in some detail. Even when initiated with substantial support from some segments of the public, educational leaders typically meet resistance, often strong resistance, from other segments of the public. Many reforms have died as the result of parental opposition.

Despite some rhetoric to the contrary, decisions about the instruction provided by schools are determined largely by the professionals, in spite of the role of school boards and the various advisory processes they have established or endorsed. The expectation (both legal and cultural) for public involvement exists; its potential should be realized and grasped. Parents have a direct role in educating their children and an indirect role through shaping the public education they receive.

## Teacher Communication with Parents and Others

The commonly expressed ideal is that the schools will have strong parental support, teachers and parents will communicate with each other in meaningful ways, and students' formal schooling will be relevant to their life outside the school. Reality, of course, is not always the same as the ideal. The interface between students' lives inside and outside the school is important and worthy of examination.

With respect to parents, the ideal is that they will be supportive of the work that teachers do with their children, communicate with teachers about their children's academic progress, and work with their children to further the work of the teachers. Teachers probably are most concerned that parents support them with respect to fostering a work ethic and a high level of student responsibility. Actual parental assistance in doing their school work is often promoted among younger children but becomes less common as children get older. In any case, the ideal is that teachers and parents communicate and support each other. In practice, this communication with parents is often more of an ideal than a reality, especially at the higher grade levels. It varies greatly by socioeconomic level, parents' educational level, and ethnic community.

Sometimes teacher communication with the community outside the school extends to faith communities, especially in some ethnic communities where the church is closely tied to the community at large. But by and large, such communication and collaborations are uncommon. Especially in terms of direct involvement on educational endeavors, faith communities and the public schools generally have little contact. Because of their diversity and lack of direct connection with the schools, most faith community involvement largely must come through families.

A basic question that may well be asked is what churches—or other community groups—have to do with the schools anyway. The automatic assumption may be that not only are they independent agencies, but because of the secular-religious divide, they properly should not have any connections. In some ways this is true, but in another sense they are connected. The connection is the students they share—students whose education is being fostered in both places. By and large I would not expect them to be engaged in collaborative activities, but given their simultaneous attention to the same issues—for example, fostering students' development of an informed worldview—there is much reason for them to know and appreciate what the other is doing. Given the nature of faith communities, one would expect a faith community to be fostering worldviews that fall within fairly limited boundaries, while schools within our pluralistic society must proceed with an understanding that their students come to them with quite varied worldviews already in place. Given this reality, one would expect that schools would not be attempting to change these worldviews in a particular direction so much as helping students to relate their new academic understandings to their extant worldview.

Given the realities of society and its schools, I would expect that the main connections between the public schools and faith communities would be through individual students. Teachers and other adult leaders in both contexts have many reasons to know what is occurring in the other arena and take it into account in their work. In most cases, it would seem that this knowledge would be communicated through individual students as they engage in educational and related activities in both contexts. It would be a natural outgrowth of working with students on individualized forms of education.

Teachers, however, generally must be the initiators of this information transfer, and the extent to which it occurs probably is very dependent upon the form of teaching that is practiced. The teacher who promotes individualized assignments, pursues educational goals deep enough to relate to students' worldviews, and empowers students to pursue their own understandings is more likely to encounter student thinking in these areas and have reason to take it into account. Teachers are the key to whether or not students' education will be authentic and complete.

## Guidelines for Public School Teachers

Individual teachers are the primary source of influence in this context. They are the ones who shape the teaching processes in their classroom and have the primary influence on the extent to which their teaching fosters a complete education for their students. There are many steps they can take in this regard; a number are presented here as guidelines for public school teachers in fostering a complete education.

An important step is furthering their own education with respect to the matters at hand. Reading significant books, or taking a course with respect to world religions, would be an important step for someone who is not well informed in this area, but this topical area is far from the whole picture of interest. A solid understanding of epistemologies of the teacher's subject field also is of critical importance. A science teacher, for example, as a minimum, should have taken the equivalent of a course on the nature of science that addresses the history, philosophy, and sociology of science. And in addition, it is important to have an understanding of alternative intellectual approaches that individual persons have used to integrate their understanding of science itself and broader, more encompassing worldviews. Of central importance in all of this is an understanding of alternative worldviews and their connection to varied cultural viewpoints and intellectual currents.

The furthering of one's education should extend to pedagogy. There is much to be learned about various approaches to engaging students in the intellectual pursuits under consideration here. The alternative approaches are many and they need to be considered in the context of the very specific goals the teacher is attempting to reach. For success, the teacher needs to engage students in new roles and engage them in new forms of student work that extend well beyond the traditional. Teachers need to be able to engage students in alternative ways of integrating their understandings acquired through different academic disciplines. It is one of the most fundamental of pedagogical tasks, but it also is often a part of the teacher's "toolkit" that is not well developed. It deserves the highest-priority attention.

Success in the educational pursuits advocated here demands that teachers develop relationships with students in which they honor their students' varied perspectives about integrating their understandings from the different academic fields, as well as the varied worldviews with which they enter the classroom. It is a matter of positive personal relationships as well as intellectual humility about one's personal grasp of intellectual modes of thinking. Both the pursuit of positive means of relating to other people and the development of intellectual depth are lifelong goals for most people. They need to be encouraged and their importance recognized.

Finally, teachers need to communicate with parents, individually and sometimes in collected groups, concerning the goals of intellectual development and integration of understandings. Parents need to understand the school's goals in this regard, how these goals will be pursued, and how this education relates to family interests and those of the faith communities they represent. In most cases, parents are not well educated in this regard, and teachers need to educate them to some extent and answer questions—some of which may be rooted in concerns parents have about the education their children are receiving.

## Guidelines for Parents

It is well known that parents have a tremendous influence on the development of their children, although during their children's adolescence parents tend to have some doubts about it. But parents can have an influential role in their children's education at all ages and are in a position to exercise this influence with respect to religion and spirituality as much as in other areas. The most important areas probably are not directly related to the school program, but arise as part of the normal processes of living together. Among the matters that connect with the school program—especially at the secondary level of education—and for which parents may have an important role to play are worldview considerations. Discussion of existential questions, whether directly or in connection with events and the arts, is important and valuable. If the education of their children includes assignments that extend to life outside the school and connect with the family, parents obviously have a role to play in encouraging this work and participating in it if that is the expectation. Projects that involve personal and auto-biographical dimensions are among those for which such connections may be sought by the student.

For the parent whose family is involved in a faith community, it is an obvious place to turn to address matters of their children's education. The education programs in place there may or may not be very sophisticated when it comes to addressing explicitly matters of worldview and secularism. Matters that, when identified, are said to be very important may or may not get much direct attention. For such a parent, the matters raised in this book need as much attention in their church, mosque, synagogue (or other faith grouping) as they do in the public schools.

Communication with teachers is another potentially important step for parents to pursue. The schools generally encourage such communication and have formal mechanisms established for this purpose. Although such communication often is focused on generalities, it can be specific and relate to social and moral development as well as the strictly academic. The potential for meaningful communication about the student and his or her development is present and often can be quite meaningful if even one of the parties—parent or teacher—takes the initiative and pursues it diligently.

Parents also have a potentially valuable role to play with the schools in terms of programmatic matters, not just in terms of the work of their individual child. Significant changes in school programs do not take place without parental involvement in the process. When initiating significant changes—or just trying to decide whether or not to do so—school leaders generally establish some means of communication with parents. School leaders seek this involvement for obvious reasons, among them the fact that parental opposition can be deadly in any change process. If parents want to see religion and spirituality have a bigger place in their school, they have every reason to become involved.

Most schools have ongoing mechanisms for such parental participation, such as school and district advisory groups. Interested parents are sought to participate in the activities of such groups. They are one area where parents can gain a hearing for their ideas. If a parent has very specific programmatic changes to recommend, there probably are more direct avenues to pursue, such as conversations with curriculum directors and principals. Change comes slowly in institutions such as schools, but it has to start somewhere, and parents are a possible—though maybe unlikely—beginning point.

Change is what is being advocated here—change regarding the way in which religion and spirituality are approached in the public schools. The process of making change happen, however, is a big topic. It is the issue to which we turn our attention next.

# TWELVE
## *Educational Reform*

This book has been advocating change in American public education. While the advocated changes pertain most directly to religion and spirituality, they are grounded in other reforms having to do with making education more personal, more individual, and more complete. Educational reform in this broader sense has received widespread attention among professionals and the public in the last couple of decades. We need to examine the topic more closely.

Making the effort to discuss how religion and spirituality can be addressed more appropriately in American education assumes that meaningful change is possible. Although optimism about change is ingrained in American culture, just how realistic is it to expect that significant improvements can be made? If change in general is slow in coming, is there reason to be hopeful about very specific changes of the sort that are being advocated here? Educational change is a much studied topic and we have a fairly clear idea of what is possible and the difficulty bringing it about in our context. It is worth further consideration.

Our educational system is not static, of course, and it continues to evolve. If we look at its history we see that its organization and structure have changed greatly over the last couple of centuries. But how about the nature of the education itself? How amenable to change is it? While we cannot do a full historical review, a brief look at the last couple of decades is feasible.

A period of intense efforts at reforming education began in the early 1980s and has persisted to the time of this writing. Concerns about education captivated the public in 1983, and over the course of that year a major national report on the topic was issued essentially every month, the most prominent being *A Nation at Risk*. It was the beginning of prominence for education on the political agenda at all levels, but especially the state level. When a particular political action gained prominence and success in one place, word quickly spread to other states and soon it gained attention essentially everywhere. For example, in the mid-1980s a move emerged to raise the high school graduation requirements in science and mathematics. In several states the legislature raised the high school graduation requirement, for example, from two courses in science to three science courses. In some states, actions of this sort were taken by the state board of education. In yet other states, with a more decentralized form of educational governance, such actions were the province of local school boards, but nevertheless this change in educational policy persisted. In such states, one school board after another changed this requirement for graduation from what had been one course to two, or from two to three. A movement to increase high school graduation requirements in specific areas swept the country.

The attempts to reform education have persisted, with wave after wave of such reforms following each other. From time to time, the reforms have been measures such as increasing the length of the school day and/or year, the development of educational standards—subject area by subject area—the enablement of charter schools, and the enactment of standardized testing programs with high stakes, i.e., inadequate test scores could have repercussions for the future of schools and their teachers. The latest of these actions—high-stakes testing—seems in some ways to reflect frustration with previous efforts that did not yield immediately obvious results. The idea seems to be, either produce good results—as measured by these tests—or we will give the job of educating these particular students to someone else. If the pattern of the past two decades persists, different political actions will supplement or supplant the current ones before long.

Most of these actions have been directed toward causing educators to take actions that they would not take without political pressure, and most of them have been based on the use of the "stick" rather than the "carrot." Not surprisingly, such negative approaches do not generate great enthusiasm from professional educators. Responses often have been a passive lack of response—"this too shall pass"—or cynicism, a feeling generated by a perceived ignoring of professional input and lack of respect for their competencies. Politicians, on the other hand, have often felt a sense of frustration about changing a large, seemingly unmovable enterprise that was not getting the results they thought should be produced. Educational change—in one form or another—has been on their agenda for a long time without getting results close to what politicians had anticipated. Few are happy with the results of all these actions. The public—as measured by opinion polls—shares this general feeling of a need for change—thus the political actions—but interestingly, people typically think their particular local school is fairly good.

Meaningful change requires more than legislative action. For it to occur on a large scale, many related actions must take place over a long period of time and the professionals have to be at the center of the action. There is a body of research that gives us some important insights into what is needed for success in such endeavors, but putting them in place is exceedingly difficult. The titles of two books on the topic—taken together—seem to tell a lot of the story. One by respected, longtime researcher Seymour Sarason titled *The Predictable Failure of Educational Reform* (1990) tells us much about the intractable nature of both the educational establishment and the problems it faces. The other side of the story—shall we say the half-full rather than the half-empty version—is captured by the title of an important book by scholars David Tyack and Larry Cuban, *Tinkering toward Utopia* (1995). Their historical perspective shows how over time the establishment does change—albeit very gradually—toward a system that is closer to our vision. Obviously, change is not easy. It takes a concerted effort, by the right people, with adequate resources and public support over a long period of time.

## Research on Educational Reform

There is an extensive body of research on educational change. Taken together, it produces a fairly strong consensus about the change process. For the person who is interested enough in the topic to tackle an entire book on it, a recent one by Michael Fullan (2001) stands at the head of the class. It is the third edition of *The New Meaning of Educational Change*. When is the last time the third edition of a book produced any reaction from you but "hohum"? Having read both earlier editions of the book, I was not expecting any big surprises, but the new edition engaged me from the beginning. It was a reminder that the research of the past decade really has been significant, and Fullan truly has captured its essence.

Fullan provides a comprehensive look at the research. His review of the research of the many scholars doing work in the field goes deep—it does not just deal with surface aspects of reform, but builds upon the fundamentals. His discussion of student learning, for example, begins with close attention to the significant research done by cognitive scientists and sociologists during the past decade and moves from the common understandings generated by these two groups to addressing motivation and relationships. We will have reason to refer to several aspects of his analysis in this brief discussion of the topic.

What follows is a brief summary of some key points from the research in the field as it pertains to the topic of this book, i.e., religion and spirituality.

### Reform Is Difficult

Anyone who has conducted empirical research on change in school settings— myself included—knows that change is difficult to bring about. The required attention to a number of different things that must be done in the right combination, with the appropriate attention to context, and with the needed long-term—years, not months—commitment is staggering. The task is seemingly overwhelming. The leaders who succeed are relatively few in number, very skilled and astute, and are in it for the long haul.

## Reform Takes a Long Time

If the changes being sought are significant and address matters of deep educational importance, they will take a long time. Important changes impinge on people's basic values and beliefs—matters that do not change quickly. An anecdote from a research study I directed illustrates the point. A new science curriculum program was being initiated in a middle school. Two teachers who initially were not convinced of its merits became convinced—after two years of using the new materials—that it really was valuable for the students. Learning how to use these materials in the optimum manner, however, was not an easy task and would require considerable effort on their part. They now were convinced it was worth the effort needed on their part to make it what it should be, but they faced a problem. For the previous two years the school district had provided helpful in-service education to the teachers to assist them in using this new program, which placed quite different demands on them as teachers than previous programs had. Up to this point these teachers had not been responsive to the assistance they had been offered, but the district had assumed that two years of such assistance was all that would be needed or utilized. Now the teachers faced a dilemma. They finally were excited about the new program and wanted help in learning how to use it well—in fact sensed a strong need for it—but the in-service education was no longer available and they felt abandoned.

This anecdote illustrates not only the need for a long-term commitment to reform, but a commitment to significant support for educators pursuing in-depth change. Furthermore, it points out how change often seems to come in bits and pieces. A plan for change built on an assumed uniform pattern of change for everyone involved is unrealistic. It does not take into account the varied circumstances, prior values and beliefs, and student needs with which different teachers are faced.

## Teacher Values and Beliefs

As with other significant educational changes, the changes being advocated in this book with respect to religion and spirituality in education are not simple changes. It is not just a matter of changing some of the information in the curriculum provided to the students. It includes changes in the goals for which the content is pursued, and it requires different pedagogical approaches on the part of the teachers. Research establishes that such changes generally involve changes in what teachers value—or think is most important—in the educational enterprise, and changes in what they believe about how learning occurs and is best facilitated by teachers. It is the need for such changes that makes the over-all reform process—assuming significant reforms—so difficult.

## New Teacher Roles

To head off into substantially new educational directions generally will demand that the teacher play a somewhat different role. Role changes are not easy. To change the content of the curriculum is relatively easy; changing the teacher's role is a very different level of difficulty. The previous anecdote—about the teachers who after two years were finally committed to a new approach but then were frustrated when there was no longer in-service education to help them—is illustrative of this point. Over a period of two years some of their values and beliefs changed. They now were ready to take on the somewhat different roles that their new commitments demanded, but the assistance for them in doing so was no longer available. Other research on teachers adopting new approaches to teaching reinforces this point. Taking on a new role as a teacher is hard work.

## New Student Roles and Work

The real changes being sought are with students. Changes in teacher values, beliefs, and roles are only a means to an end. The desired student changes are matters of student outcomes—although not just those that can be measured with tests—but the means of getting to these new outcomes are probably a result of the students taking on new roles and engaging in new forms of student work. An illustration of such changes—for both teachers and students—is contained in the following table produced in one of our research projects (Anderson, 1996). It displays what we labeled "traditional" and "reform" patterns of education as displayed in a study of schools actively engaged in the process of making changes across the various curricular areas. While not derived from a study directed toward religion and spirituality, it does present a picture of what significant educational change entails.

## Traditional-Reform Continuum

Table 1

| Predominance of Old Orientation | Predominance of New Orientation |
|---|---|
| **Teacher Role** | **Teacher Role** |
| <u>As dispenser of knowledge</u> | <u>As coach and facilitator</u> |
| · Transmits information | · Helps students process info. |
| · Communicates with individuals | · Communicates with groups |
| · Directs student actions | · Coaches student actions |
| · Explains conceptual relationships | · Facilitates student thinking |
| · Teacher's knowledge is static | · Models the learning process |
| · Directed use of textbook, etc. | · Flexible use of materials |
| **Student Role** | **Student Role** |
| <u>As passive receiver</u> | <u>As self-directed learner</u> |
| · Records teacher's information | · Processes information |
| · Memorizes information | · Interprets, explains, hypothesizes |
| · Follows teacher's directions | · Designs own activities |
| · Defers to teacher as authority | · Shares authority for answers |
| **Student Work** | **Student Work** |
| <u>Teacher-prescribed activities</u> | <u>Student-directed learning</u> |
| · Completes worksheets | · Directs own learning |
| · All students complete same tasks | · Tasks vary among students |
| · Teacher directs tasks | · Designs and directs own tasks |
| · Absence of items on right | ·Emphasizes reasoning, reading and writing for meaning, solving problems, building from existing cognitive structures, and explaining complex problems |

This display summarizes fairly well differences in orientations to teaching and learning described in chapter 2. The nature of the students' roles and of the type of work in which they are engaged varies greatly. Furthermore, to change the situation for the students from the more traditional one to the reform version demands a very different role for the teacher—a change that is not easy to make.

We have yet to address what can be done to move from a traditional emphasis to an approach with more of the reform emphasis, and we also need to look more closely at the type of changes described above in Table 1 with focused attention on the matters of religion and spirituality developed in this book. Before doing either, however, it would be well to examine current educational reform in the United States.

## Current Educational Reforms

It is obvious that many value judgments are embedded in the Traditional-Reform Continuum displayed above. The reform side of the continuum reflects both the intentions of the reformers being studied in that research project and the actual classroom practices found in the classes of the teachers who were pursuing these reforms. But we are still left with the question of why they were pursuing these particular reforms. The schools selected to be part of that collection of case studies were ones that were committed to implementing the reforms advocated in national standards documents such as those of the National Council of Teachers of Mathematics or the National Research Council or those of whatever particular curricular area pertained. The intended reforms were consistent with those practices reflected in our earlier discussion of teaching for understanding, the results of cognitive science research about human learning, multiple intelligences, and related matters. While none of the reforms advocated in the various national standards were without controversy, there has been a fairly strong consensus about moving toward educational goals and pedagogical practices of this type.

While reforms of this type have been moving ahead—albeit slowly and on a broken front—other reform efforts prominent early in the twenty-first century appear to be having a counteractive effect. We have arrived at a point as of this writing where a convergence of state and national political actions has yielded a mandated system of standardized testing based on specified standards. In spite of rhetoric to the contrary, cost factors are usually yielding tests that are machine scorable. As a result, standards that may have started out as thoughtful and potentially very helpful—such as the *NCTM Math Standards* and the *National Science Education Standards*—are transmogrified through the testing programs into shallow and narrow definitions of education. Since the tests are "high stakes"—i.e., there are serious repercussions for schools, administrators, and teachers if scores are low—the educational process is changed to increase test scores rather than focus on education more broadly.

As a person who has been a promoter of educational reform and who has spent much of an educational career studying and researching educational change, it is disappointing to see these developments. Many efforts at reform have had positive results but this turn is in the opposite direction. The curriculum is being "dumbed down" and teaching approaches are moving toward the dull and deadening. My negative judgment on these developments is independent of my interest in the place of religion and spirituality in education, but the current turn toward standards-based, high-stakes testing creates a problematic context in which to address matters of religion and spirituality in schools. Aside from what it was intended to accomplish, this rush to high-stakes testing is having a strong impact—probably unintended—on both curriculum content and teaching practices. Because of what it is feasible to measure with standardized tests—at least those that are financially viable—the curriculum is becoming narrowed considerably and the teaching practices that are perceived to be most effective for this content—a lot of drill and practice—are increasingly prominent. This move toward a dumbed-down curriculum and deadening teaching approaches is described seemingly everywhere by teachers facing the new testing programs. Current political actions in many cases are running counter to what the results of research indicate would be wise actions.

This phenomenon is important to take into account as we consider the relationship between the overall educational reform movement and our consideration of the place of religion and spirituality in education. The directions in which reform had been moving prior to the full flowering of the testing movement are very consistent with what has been advocated here about religion and spirituality in education. A focus on individuality and student pursuit of their personal understanding of spirituality in the context of various curricular topics, self-directed learning, and individual student designing of their own learning activities are all consistent with giving attention to spirituality and personal religious matters. As the testing movement comes to the fore, however, it would appear that educational reform is taking on a flavor that will make our goal harder to attain.

## Putting Reform into Practice

Reform can be addressed at many levels, such as through national or state political action, or school district – level policy changes initiated by the school board. Change also can be the result of administrative actions under the leadership of the superintendent or at the school level under the leadership of the principal. The most fundamental changes, however, occur with teachers them-selves. Although other levels are not irrelevant, for purposes of the renewed attention to religion and spirituality under consideration here, teachers are the main focus, given the centrality of the teaching process itself. Teachers, more than curriculum developers and other supervisory personnel, are the ones who are in a position to make the proposed changes. In this regard, initial teacher preparation programs play a central role, a topic to which we will return later. Assistance for currently employed teachers, however, is also a matter of importance.

### Teacher Assistance

With respect to such assistance, Fullan (2001) has described the situation very well:

> Significant educational change consists of changes in beliefs, teaching style, and materi-als, which can come about *only* through a process of personal development in a social context. (p. 124)

He is describing the kind of changes that have been our focus here, and he puts the emphasis on personal development for teachers, which he says must occur in a "social context." The research is quite clear on this point. Teacher collabo-ration is powerful as a means of personal development for teachers. While for-mal education sessions for teachers can provide a strong social context, the most powerful is a work context where teachers work together on the actual teaching issues. The ideal setting for teachers to address the issues of how to give more appropriate attention to religion and spirituality in their teaching is in a collaborative work context where they can work together to modify teaching approaches and adapt teaching materials to have the desired results. Within such a context, new values and beliefs on the part of teachers can be expected to emerge.

While teacher development is a central matter, it must be emphasized that it is not just an individual matter; it is a systems issue:

> We are talking about *reculturing* the teaching profession—the process of creating and fostering purposeful learning communities. (p. 136)

A new set of norms and expectations is needed.

### A Public Consensus

The desired assistance for teachers is unlikely to be provided, however, in the absence of a public consensus on the importance of this attention to religion and spirituality in education. The probability of such a consensus developing is hard to gauge. The rather sudden appearance of a number of books on the topic of religion in education during the last decade is an indication of growing interest (e.g., Nord, 1995; Nord and Haynes, 1998; Noddings 1993; Fraser, 1999; Nash, 1999), but the influence of other factors may be in either direction. The growing retreat from public education of some religiously inclined people into private schools and home schooling could, on the one hand, be indicative of a loss of people with these interests from the public school arena or, on the other hand, could be a stimulus to the public schools to recognize an unmet need. Whatever the nature of these and other influences, unless some public consensus emerges, a substantial change is unlikely.

## Family and Faith Community Participation

For educational reform in general, parental participation has been a strong influence, both positively and negatively. While in many cases parents have been very supportive of reforms, in many other cases they have become critical and begun to actively oppose reforms once they were under way. The most common form of such opposition probably has been from parents—generally of higher socioeconomic status—who are especially concerned about their children's preparation for and admission to college and are convinced that traditional forms of curricula and teaching are the most certain means of reaching this goal. Parents may support or oppose educational reforms.

Parental interest in greater attention to religion is a speculative matter. Greater—more balanced—attention to religion in the curriculum—for instance, in world history—is unlikely to be a controversial matter. On the other hand, it is hard to judge parental response to the more personal and autobiographical focus on religion and spirituality advocated here. Some of the more conservative religious parents may be apprehensive, not trusting the schools to get close to personal religious matters.

The most important dimension of parental involvement may be in connection with the personal and autobiographical aspects of this education. With such an approach it would be well to encourage students—when the students themselves are comfortable with it—to pursue discussions with their parents about what they are doing in this regard in school. The same would be true of student conversations with others in their faith community if they are part of one.

The key in the type of educational reform advocated here is student empowerment and initiative in pursuing their own learning and understanding. They must be in the driver's seat. The integrated learning they are pursuing potentially involves the family and faith community, but the students are the ones who will determine the extent to which this involvement with others will occur. The schools must not be in a position of pressing for such engagement,

The schools must not be in a position of pressing for such engagement, but should be encouragers and facilitators of this personal learning when students are so inclined.

## The Changes Sought

The changes under consideration here are specific ones related to religion and spirituality in education. One is largely a matter of curricular change, i.e., changing the content of the curriculum to include appropriate attention to matters of religion in places where it rightfully belongs. The prime example, of course, is inclusion of the influence of religion on history. The second major item is more pedagogical than curricular. It is a matter of teacher practices creating a hospitable classroom climate, honoring all student viewpoints, encouraging student exploration of existential questions, and other aspects of instruction that impinge on students' personal understandings of religious and spiritual matters. Both the curricular and instructional aspects are important, but they may be quite different from each other in terms of how change should be sought.

Two examples of curricular change are useful for our consideration. One would be the addition to the school curriculum of courses such as those recommended by Warren Nord. As noted earlier, his preferred option is the addition to the high school curriculum of a three-course sequence including World Religions, Religion and Modernity, and Moral Philosophy. His minimum option is a course required of all students that is focused on the central themes of the above three courses. The second curricular approach would be to give these topics their due within existing courses in the school curriculum, such as courses in world history, U.S. history, and current social issues. The two examples are quite different from each other in terms of what is required to bring them about. The former is largely a matter of formal changes in the course offerings of a school reached by going through an institutional process. The latter approach demands working with a larger number of teachers and calls for changes in how they handle their work within the courses they currently teach. In this regard, this form of curricular change has some similarity to pedagogical changes which will be discussed below. The two forms of curricular change discussed here are very different in terms of how the changes would be brought about, what the prospects for success are, and the resulting impact on students' education.

In chapter 6 three dimensions of education in religion and spirituality were described: (1) curricular content as illustrated by the Nord proposals, (2) spirituality as a focus of classroom discourse with the Kessler proposals as an exemplar, and (3) faith commitments or "life wagers" described in the language of Fowler. The first of these three was addressed above in our consideration of curricular changes. The latter two are more closely connected to pedagogical changes. In many ways they are more difficult and complicated than curricular changes. It is not just a matter of deciding that a particular course will be included or excluded, or selecting particular topics within a course. Pedagogical changes—such as how teachers relate to students, the role teachers play, and the expectations teachers have for students—have many facets and are not easy to bring about.

The nature of these pedagogical changes, and the manner in which they realistically can be expected to occur, are such that it is difficult to be effective as a parent or any other "outsider" in initiating them. Such fundamental changes in the way teachers do their work almost always involve changes in teachers' values about what is important in education and changes in their beliefs about how students learn and how schools should operate. Changes of this nature will not happen as a direct result of parents lobbying the schools.

Pedagogical changes of this nature can come about only through intensive examination of personal teaching practices by teachers themselves—an examination done in a collaborative context with other teachers, with administrative support for such changes, and adequate and appropriate resources for the process. Thus, to be effective, any lobbying for, and encouragement of, this sort of change must be focused on long-term changes and on establishing realistic mechanisms to promote change, and be done in cooperation with teachers themselves. The first step is communication.

Any parent or parent group wishing to consider such actions would be well advised to make use of resources available from organizations such as the First Amendment Center at Vanderbilt University, which has a direct interest in these issues. Information about them is available on the Internet at www.freedomforum.org. A project they are cosponsoring with the Association for Supervision and Curriculum Development may be of particular interest. They have established a grant program to create model school programs in which schools will teach First Amendment principles and model these principles. Information about this program is available at www.firstamendmentschools.org. One of their publications which has been widely distributed, *A Parent's Guide to Religion in the Public Schools*, also is available at this Web site.

This latter section of the chapter has been written as if it were directed to parents and public groups. But much of what has been said here applies to educators as well. In particular, any educators planning initiatives in this arena would be well advised to seek the widest possible involvement of parent groups. School leaders should seek family and faith community collaboration. These community people should not be seen as a threat, nor should their participation be seen as just a political necessity. They can be positive contributors to the endeavor.

## A Long-Term Commitment

The public consensus to which reference was made above must be translated into a long-term goal on the part of policymakers and other leaders if substantial reform is to occur. The statement on the role of religion in education which was released in 1995 and again in 1998 by Secretary of Education Riley during the Clinton administration is an example of an important move on the part of policymakers. But many other actions will be necessary and they must be sustained over a long time span. An example of action is changes in teacher education, a topic worthy of more extended treatment in the following chapter.

# THIRTEEN
## *Teacher Education*

In our previous discussion of educational reform, considerable attention was given to support for teachers who are attempting to initiate new educational approaches—including both support in the context of the ongoing work setting and formal in-service education classes. While the term *in-service education* commonly is reserved for formal classes for teachers, in fact, some of the most valuable education occurs in the context of collaborative on-the-job work with fellow teachers. This matter was addressed in the previous chapter, and at this point we can move on to the other major category of teacher education—initial teacher preparation.

Teacher education and the related initial certification process carry high expectations in our social and political context—expectations that probably are unrealistic. It is widely thought that if teacher education were just done correctly, the schools would soon be staffed by teachers with high levels of professional competence. Our prior discussion of in-service education and all that is required to enable teachers to address their personal educational values and beliefs in hopes of changing their educational practices should offer some insights about how difficult the task is. As the old shibboleth says, "Teachers teach as they were taught," and the process of preparing them to teach in a different manner is far more complex than it appears on the surface. Teachers who adopt an approach to religion and spirituality consistent with the vision presented in this book probably will gain a major part of the necessary competencies in a school context after they have completed their initial preparation.

Even though expectations for initial teacher education probably are unrealistically high, much can be accomplished at that point and such programs play an important role in preparing new teachers to join the teacher workforce and begin offering quality education to students. It appears, however, that with respect to the issue at hand—religion and spirituality in education—teacher education programs—including many top-quality ones—could make some significant improvements. It is these changes to which we turn our attention now.

The teacher education advocated here is a quality program in the conventional sense with a few key modifications and additions. These alterations to the standard programs as usually found across the country are three in number and affect different aspects of the standard program. The first proposal is the addition of a minimum of one course in religious studies for all teacher certification students. The second is a modification of the preparation in multicultural education that typically is provided. Finally, changes are suggested in the pedagogical training of teacher education students.

## Religious Studies

The recommendation by Nord (1995) that religious studies departments offer courses for prospective teachers which address matters of religion in the public school, in my judgment, is sound. He suggests one general course and a set of others that are specific to the issues of literature, social studies, and science. He would prefer that all teachers take the general one and that teachers of the three specific fields take the one for their specific teaching area in addition. He wants these courses available but does not say they should be required: He says the prospective teachers should be encouraged to take them. I would argue for the one general course, knowing how much competition there is for space in a teacher preparation program. If properly designed, this course could give teachers helpful background for dealing with religious issues in many aspects of schooling. While this background would be more important for teachers in some areas (e.g., history) than in others, it would be important for all teachers, since the matters of religion and spirituality we have been considering impinge on all parts of the curriculum.

This requirement would be harder to implement in most teacher education programs than it may appear on the surface because of the strong competition for the time—that is the credit hours—available. There has been strong political pressure in many places to reduce the number of credit hours required for certification, and with the current shortage of certified teachers in so many locations—especially in certain teaching fields—the pressure is intensifying. As good and reasonable as the proposal is, it still faces a severe uphill struggle. Nevertheless, the recommendation is very modest and reasonable, and deserving of serious attention on the part of those persons having influence in these arenas.

## Multicultural Education

Another change that should be initiated in teacher education programs is to give greater attention to religion within those portions of the program pertaining to multicultural education. Most teacher education programs have at least a major portion of a course which focuses on this topic, including matters of race, ethnicity, gender, sexual orientation, and other personal characteristics related to the great diversity of our society. Although religion obviously is a significant factor among these characteristics that make our society so diverse, it tends not to be one that is given much attention in this context. It should be.

A conversation with students in one of my classes a couple of years ago may illustrate the situation. It was a small class of currently employed teachers who were mostly fairly new in the profession and were also pursuing a master's degree. It was a special topics course offered on a one-time basis titled Religion, Spirituality, and Education. Well along in the course—after most of the issues were on the table and the students were aware of the legal issues and the compelling reasons for attending to religion in education—one of the students suddenly launched into a personal concern with considerable passion. Referring to an initial teacher program she had completed only a year or two before, she said something like the following: "Why have I never heard about all of this before? In my teacher education program almost nothing was ever said about religion, yet every time I turned around I was hearing about multiculturalism. My religion is a more important part of who I am than my ethnicity. How could they have ignored it?" An audible comment or two and body language in the group indicated she had hit a responsive chord. My first thought was that she was challenging the attention to multiculturalism and diversity in her program, but that was not the point. Her point was that the persons operating the program could not really have understood and had a commitment to multiculturalism and diversity if they had such myopia. She felt her program had been inadequate and clearly below standard in this regard.

The conversation did not end there. This class was fairly diverse in a religious sense, with students having various religious affiliations and some with none at all—"I'm spiritual but not religious." We had been quite open with each other from the beginning as to who we were in this sense, and the student who launched into the aforementioned commentary was one who had identified herself as a Christian. She went on to say that as a religious person she felt excluded from consideration in many class discussions. The words that finally surfaced to describe what she and a number of others experienced were "marginalized" and "stereotyped."

The feeling of being marginalized may be obvious from what has already been said. Topics were pursued as if religion was not a significant consideration for anyone in her class on a personal basis nor was it relevant in a social or educational sense to whatever issue was under discussion at the moment. The feeling of being stereotyped was due to the way in which educational issues were addressed when religion did enter the conversation. Whenever a set of categories was employed to describe alternative educational ideologies—such as traditional, progressive, and radical—a religious perspective seemingly was automatically equated with "traditional." An analogous situation would be if, in using Eisner's (1992) six categories of curriculum ideologies mentioned in chapter 5, any religious orientation was automatically categorized as "religious orthodoxy."

One may ask how common the type of teacher education experience just described is in programs across the country. I know of no survey data that would give an answer to that question, but based on informal interactions and conversations such as the one in the class described above, I do not think it uncommon.

If the situation is common, it is extremely unfortunate because it conveys by example to teacher education students how religion should be handled in elementary and secondary schools when new teachers get on the job. Furthermore, it means the program is failing to do in a proactive manner the task it is committed to doing—preparing teachers to teach in a multicultural and diverse society.

Taking multiculturalism seriously is a key to giving religion its rightful place in the schools. America is religiously diverse and this societal fact is foundational to any approach to addressing religion appropriately in our democratic society. In understanding this situation more fully, a useful distinction is one made in an earlier chapter between secularization and secularism. (This distinction has been made by a number of authors including Harvey Cox—as cited in Fraser, 1999, p. 233—and Huston Smith, 2001). The former is a cultural phenomenon that history shows to be one of the most important themes of modern history. This secularization is correlated with our pluralism and diversity. Given our religious diversity, our democratic society has to operate in the public square on a largely secular basis even though we are also a very religious society. Thus, we are both a very secular and a very religious society.

This secularization, however, is very different from the ideology of secularism which in effect removes considerations of the divine from any human endeavor. Secularism has a place at the table with other religions and ideologies. The difficulty that arises in our multicultural society is when secularism becomes the operating ideology of the schools by excluding religious perspectives from view. Any supposedly full multicultural consideration of educational issues that does not include attention to religious diversity is by default installing secularism as the dominant worldview and in effect repudiating the very multiculturalism it supposedly is promoting for our democratic society.

An excellent resource for a person teaching a class on multiculturalism in public education would be the book by James W. Fraser (1999) titled *Between*

*Church and State*, with a subtitle of *Religion & Public Education in a Multicultural America*. It provides a sound historical, cultural, and legal analysis of the overall situation and draws out the implications for addressing contemporary educational issues. While there are other resources, this one stands out for me as a resource concerning religion as an aspect of multicultural education in America.

On the surface at least, it would seem easier to make teacher education what it should be in this regard than the change advocated earlier, namely adding a course in religious studies to a person's program. After all, it does not mean adding a course to the program. It only means modifying an existing course—where needed—to make it what it should be. The question is whether or not the persons teaching such courses are convinced of the point being made here and are prepared to make the necessary changes in cases where they are needed. My answers to the question are very speculative in that I do not have a broad base of information about the content of such courses nor the ideological commitments of the people teaching them across the country.

### Pedagogical Preparation

Education in how to go about the practice of teaching is embedded in most parts of a teacher education program, including those portions devoted to multiculturalism. Thus, there is no one place in the typical teacher education program to turn to find where the specifics of the teaching act are addressed. Some aspects are addressed in what are often called foundation courses, but the majority is found in classes focused on the teaching process itself—sometimes called methods courses—either courses devoted specifically to a particular subject area, such as language arts, social studies, science, or mathematics, or a course aimed at the teaching process in general.

Courses directed to teaching a specific subject area generally assume a background in the subject field on the part of the students before they get to this course. In my personal experience, students coming into a course on teaching middle school and high school science have already had a full major in one of the natural sciences, e.g., biology, geology, chemistry, or physics, and the introductory freshman year courses in the other major areas of the natural sciences. It is typical of secondary school teacher education programs across the country for students to be required to have a major in the field they are teaching. This does not mean, however, that these students have had a course that deals with the philosophical underpinnings of the field and the methodologies employed in its research. Although our secondary school science education students are required to have a course that addresses the history and philosophy of science, this is not typical of programs across the country. Continuing with science as our example, such a course is helpful in preparing students to address the controversy over teaching evolution as discussed in chapter 7. There is a need to address the issue in the course on teaching science, just as other specific issues unique to each subject field must be addressed in the analogous teacher education course.

Another aspect of the teaching process could be addressed in a general course on teaching as well as in a specific subject-oriented course, namely the autobiographical approach to teaching that has been advocated in this book. Teachers intending to use such approaches would find preparation for doing so very helpful. It must be built into courses on teaching, although in this day of high-stakes testing, it may not seem as imperative to some people as it once may have. It needs attention in any general course on teaching and further consideration in the context of teaching specific subjects such as literature.

This preparation to use such approaches should extend into the field experiences of the teacher education students, i.e., their practicum experiences in the schools and student teaching. There is an obvious dilemma here, one common to all attempts to instill new practices, such as some of those found in the various sets of national standards. If the practices are not already in place in the schools, there is no place to put teacher education students to experience them in the "real world." The best prospects are in student teaching settings where the cooperating teacher is open to innovation and is willing to try new approaches in the context of a collaborative relationship with personnel from the teacher education program.

As a closing point, it is well to keep constantly in mind that in all aspects of teacher education, the values and beliefs we are seeking are at the heart of the matter. We are not simply addressing techniques or "methods," we are dealing with particular visions for what education should be and what we want students to become in our diverse, plural, democratic society. A part of this process is for prospective teachers to come to understand themselves, including their worldview and how it shapes who they are as persons and teachers. With this personal focus we have the potential of educating teachers who can give religion and spirituality their proper place in the public school curriculum.

# FOURTEEN
## *Epilogue*

My goal has been to make a case for a new approach to public education that gives religion and spirituality the enhanced role they deserve. The intent is that they have this role within the context of education that is complete for all students: religious and nonreligious, believers and skeptics, spiritual and nonspiritual. It is an ideal, a reasonable goal, and worth the effort required to make significant progress in this direction. There is an answer to the dilemma posed by our society with its combination of religious and secular orientations.

As believers in both democracy and religious freedom, we face a challenge. We often need to be able to accommodate strong beliefs on the part of others which we think are deeply misguided. If schools are to be communities that support and celebrate diversity in the full sense, we must be prepared to accept and support beliefs we find disturbing. Within our schools we want neither culture wars, nor a hypocrisy that pretends differences do not exist, nor the imposition of an alternative metaphysics that suppresses ideas which may be perceived as misguided. It is a challenging task, but one with great potential benefits. The goal is not just to resolve the dilemma posed so often in this book, but to reach some important goals for our society, schools, and students.

The eventual societal goal espoused here is a society that supports and celebrates diversity in its many forms. The goal is a society that is *civil,* i.e., a society that accommodates its diversity with as little conflict as possible, and finds its commonality in the fact that it is comprised of people having great particularity on many dimensions, including religion and understandings of spirituality.

As a result, the goal for our schools is a sense of community that mirrors the goal espoused for society at large. The school community should support and celebrate diversity, handle conflicts in a civil manner, and foster community that is grounded in particularity. Furthermore, this orientation should be intellectually grounded, i.e., this diversity must be understood in terms of its history, cultures, and worldviews.

The goal for students is that they experience this community in such a manner that they are comfortable with their uniqueness—first of all recognizing it and then experiencing support and respect for whatever their particular uniqueness is. Within this school community, of course, they should be supported in gaining an intellectual grounding for understanding their uniqueness. They should grow in their understanding of the various epistemologies operative in their lives and the manner in which they personally integrate the understandings coming from these varied sources.

If these individual student goals are attained, we can expect progress in gaining our desired society. Individual student gains cycle back to the benefit of society as a whole. If our society gains the preferred schools, we can expect that the results among students will influence them to become adults that seek what we desire for society as a whole. Turning this ideal into some significant amount of reality is a challenging endeavor. I proceed with the expectation that we are up to the challenge.

# APPENDIX

---

This appendix contains an unabridged reproduction of a statement from the Freedom Forum First Amendment Center titled *A Teacher's Guide to Religion in the Public Schools*. While the content has a lot of similarity to statements released by the U.S. Department of Education under the administrations of both President William Clinton and President George W. Bush, this one has the advantages of being especially well-organized and well-written, complete in its coverage and free from any inference of partisan emphasis. The endorsements of the statement by a wide range of religious and educational organizations also show there is strong consensus support for this expression of the situation. Taken together—this statement plus the statements from the administrations of two different parties—they show the unanimity of legal, political, and social opinion about the necessary and appropriate place of religion in America's public schools. *A Teacher's Guide to Religion in the Public Schools* is published by the First Amendment Center.

The guide has been endorsed by the following organizations:

American Association of School Administrators, American Federation of Teachers, American Jewish Committee, American Jewish Congress, Anti-Defamation League, Association for Supervision and Curriculum Development, Baptist Joint Committee on Public Affairs, Catholic League for Religious and Civil Rights, Christian Educators Association International, Christian Legal Society, Council on Islamic Education, National Association of Elementary School Principals, National Association of Evangelicals, National Association of Secondary School Principals, National Council of Churches of Christ in the U.S.A., National Council for the Social Studies, National Education Association, National PTA, National School Boards Association, Union of American Hebrew Congregations, and Union of Orthodox Jewish Congregations of America.

## A Teacher's Guide to Religion in the Public Schools

"Congress shall make no law respecting an establishment of religion, or prohibiting the free exercise thereof ..."

Religion Clauses of the First Amendment to the U.S. Constitution

Each day millions of parents from diverse religious backgrounds entrust the education of their children to the teachers in our nation's public schools. For this reason, teachers need to be fully informed about the constitutional and educational principles for understanding the role of religion in public education.

This teacher's guide is intended to move beyond the confusion and conflict that has surrounded religion in public schools since the early days of the common school movement. For most of our history, extremes have shaped much of the debate. On one end of the spectrum are those who advocate promotion of religion (usually their own) in school practices and policies. On the other end are those who view public schools as religion-free zones. Neither of these approaches is consistent with the guiding principles of the Religion Clauses of the First Amendment.

Fortunately, however, there is another alternative that is consistent with the First Amendment and broadly supported by many educational and religious groups. The core of this alternative has been best articulated in "Religious Liberty, Public Education, and the Future of American Democracy," a statement of principles issued by 24 national organizations. Principle IV states:

> Public schools may not inculcate nor inhibit religion. They must be places where religion and religious conviction are treated with fairness and respect. Public schools uphold the First Amendment when they protect the religious liberty rights of students of all faiths or none. Schools demonstrate fairness when they ensure that the curriculum includes study about religion, where appropriate, as an important part of a complete education.[1]

The questions and answers that follow build on this shared vision of religious liberty in public education to provide teachers with a basic understanding

---

[1] This shared vision of religious liberty in public education is remarkable both for who says it and for what it says. The National Education Association, the American Federation of Teachers, the National School Boards Association, the Association for Supervision and Curriculum Development, the National PTA and the American Association of School Administrators join with the Christian Legal Society, the American Center for Law and Justice, and Citizens for Excellence in Education in asserting these principles. People for the American Way, the Anti-Defamation League and the Union of American Hebrew Congregations are on the list, as are the Council on Islamic Education and the Christian Educators Association International, and the Christian Coalition. Free copies are available through the First Amendment Center.

of the issues concerning religion in their classrooms. The advice offered is based on First Amendment principles as currently interpreted by the courts and agreed to by a wide range of religious and educational organizations. For a more in-depth examination of the issues, teachers should consult *Finding Common Ground: A First Amendment Guide to Religion and Public Education.*[2] This guide is not intended to render legal advice on specific legal questions; it is designed to provide general information on the subject of religion and public schools.

Keep in mind, however, that the law alone cannot answer every question. Teachers and administrators, working with parents and others in the community, must work to apply the First Amendment fairly and justly for all students in our public schools.

### 1. Is it Constitutional to Teach about Religion?

Yes. In the 1960s school prayer cases (that prompted rulings against state-sponsored school prayer and Bible reading), the U.S. Supreme Court indicated that public school education may include teaching about religion. In *Abington v. Schempp,* Associate Justice Tom Clark wrote for the Court:

> [I]t might well be said that one's education is not complete without a study of comparative religion or the history of religion and its relationship to the advancement of civilization. It certainly may be said that the Bible is worthy of study for its literary and historic qualities. Nothing we have said here indicates that such study of the Bible or of religion, when presented objectively as part of a secular program of education, may not be effected consistently with the First Amendment.

### 2. Why Should Study about Religion be Included in the Curriculum?

Growing numbers of educators throughout the United States recognize that study about religion in social studies, literature, art, and music is an important part of a well-rounded education. "Religion in the Public School Curriculum: Questions and Answers," issued by a coalition of 17 major religious and educational organizations—including the Christian Legal Society, the American Jewish Congress, the National Education Association, the American Federation of Teachers, the American Association of School Administrators, the Islamic Society of North America, the National Council for the Social Studies, the Association for Supervision and Curriculum Development, the Baptist Joint Committee on Public Affairs, the National Association of Evangelicals, and the National

---

[2] *Finding Common Ground* by Charles C. Haynes and Oliver Thomas is available at cost from the First Amendment Center. Call (615) 321-9588.

School Boards Association—describes the importance of religion in the curriculum thus:

> Because religion plays a significant role in history and society, study about religion is essential to understanding both the nation and the world. Omission of facts about religion can give students the false impression that the religious life of humankind is insignificant or unimportant. Failure to understand even the basic symbols, practices, and concepts of the various religions makes much of history, literature, art, and contemporary life unintelligible.
>
> Study about religion is also important if students are to value religious liberty, the first freedom guaranteed in the Bill of Rights. Moreover, knowledge of the roles of religion in the past and present promotes cross-cultural understanding essential to democracy and world peace.

A number of leading educational groups have issued their own statements decrying the lack of discussion about religion in the curriculum and calling for inclusion of such information in curricular materials and in teacher education.

Three major principles form the foundation of this consensus on teaching about religion in public schools:

1. As the Supreme Court has made clear, study about religion in public schools is constitutional.

2. Inclusion of study about religion is important in order for students to be properly educated about history and cultures.

3. Religion must be taught objectively and neutrally. The purpose of public schools is to educate students about a variety of religious traditions, not to indoctrinate them into any tradition.

### 3. Is Study about Religion Included in Textbooks and Standards?

"Knowledge about religions is not only characteristic of an educated person, but is also absolutely necessary for understanding and living in a world of diversity."

National Council for the Social Studies

Agreement on the importance of teaching about religion has begun to influence the treatment of religion in textbooks widely used in public schools, as well as state frameworks and standards for the social studies. The current generation of history textbooks mention religion more often than their predecessors, and, in world history, sometimes offer substantive discussions of religious ideas and events.

State frameworks and standards are also beginning to treat religion more seriously. Most state standards in the social studies require or recommend teaching about religion through specific content references and general mandates, and many also include such references in fine arts and literature standards. In California, for example, the History-Social Science Framework and the new History-Social Science Content Standards require considerable study of religion. Students studying U.S. History in California are expected to learn about the role of religion in the American story, from the influence of religious groups on social reform movements to the religious revivals, from the rise of Christian fundamentalism to the expanding religious pluralism of the 20th century.

Teaching about religion is also encouraged in the *National Standards for History*, published by the National Center for History in the Schools. The elaborated standards in world history are particularly rich in religious references, examining the basic beliefs and practices of the major religions as well as how these faiths influenced the development of civilization in successive historical periods. While the U.S. history standards include religion less frequently, many historical developments and contributions that were influenced by religion are nevertheless represented.

*Geography for Life: The National Geography Standards*, published by the Geography Standards Project, and the *National Standards for Civics and Government*, published by the Center for Civic Education, include many references to teaching about religious belief and practice as historical and contemporary phenomena. Study of religion in the social studies would be expanded considerably if curriculum developers and textbook writers were guided by these standards.

## 4. How Should I Teach about Religion?

Encouraged by the new consensus, public schools are now beginning to include more teaching about religion in the curriculum. In the social studies especially, the question is no longer "Should I teach about religion?" but rather "How should I do it?"

The answer to the "how" question begins with a clear understanding of the crucial difference between the teaching of religion (religious education or indoctrination) and teaching about religion. "Religion in the Public School Curriculum," the guidelines issued by 17 religious and educational organizations, summarizes the distinction this way:

· The school's approach to religion is *academic*, not *devotional.*
· The school strives for student *awareness* of religions, but does not press for student *acceptance* of any religion.

· The school sponsors study *about* religion, not the *practice* of religion.
· The school may *expose* students to a diversity of religious views, but may not *impose* any particular view.
· The school *educates* about all religions; it does not *promote* or *denigrate* religion.
· The school *informs* students about various beliefs; it does not seek to *conform* students to any particular belief.[3]

Classroom discussions concerning religion must be conducted in an environment that is free of advocacy on the part of the teacher. Students may, of course, express their own religious views, as long as such expression is germane to the discussion. But public-school teachers are required by the First Amendment to teach about religion fairly and objectively, neither promoting nor denigrating religion in general or specific religious groups in particular. When discussing religion, many teachers guard against injecting personal religious beliefs by teaching through attribution (e.g., by using such phrases as "most Buddhists believe..." or "according to the Hebrew scriptures...").

## 5. Which Religions Should be Taught and How Much Should be Said?

Decisions about which religions to include and how much to discuss about religion are determined by the grade level of the students and the academic requirements of the course being taught.

In the elementary grades, the study of family, community, various cultures, the nation, and other themes and topics may involve some discussion of religion. Elementary students are introduced to the basic ideas and practices of the world's major religions by focusing on the generally agreed-upon meanings of religious faiths—the core beliefs and symbols as well as important figures and events. Stories drawn from various faiths may be included among the wide variety of stories read by students, but the material selected must always be presented in the context of learning about religion.

On the secondary level, the social studies, literature, and the arts offer opportunities for the inclusion of study about religions—their ideas and practices. The academic needs of the course determine which religions are studied. In a U.S. history curriculum, for example, some faith communities may be given more time than others but only because of their predominant influence on the development of the American nation. In world history, a variety of faiths are studied in each region of the world in order to understand the various civiliza-

---

[3] Based on guidelines originally published by the Public Education Religion Studies Center at Wright State University.

tions and cultures that have shaped history and society. The overall curriculum should include all of the major voices and some of the minor ones in an effort to provide the best possible education.

Fair and balanced study about religion on the secondary level includes critical thinking about historical events involving religious traditions. Religious beliefs have been at the heart of some of the best and some of the worst developments in human history. The full historical record (and various interpretations of it) should be available for analysis and discussion. Using primary sources whenever possible allows students to work directly with the historical record.

Of course, fairness and balance in U.S. or world history and literature is difficult to achieve, given the brief treatment of religious ideas and events in most textbooks and the limited time available in the course syllabus. Teachers will need scholarly supplemental resources that enable them to cover the required material within the allotted time, while simultaneously enriching the discussion with study of religion. Some schools now offer electives in religious studies in order to provide additional opportunities for students to study about the major faith communities in greater depth.

## 6. May I Invite Guest Speakers to Help with Study about Religion?

When teaching about religions in history, some teachers may find it helpful to invite a guest speaker for a more comprehensive presentation of the religious tradition under study. Teachers should consult their school district policy concerning guest speakers in the classroom.

If a guest speaker is invited, care should be taken to find someone with the academic background necessary for an objective and scholarly discussion of the historical period and the religion being considered. Faculty from local colleges and universities often make excellent guest speakers or can make recommendations of others who might be appropriate for working with students in a public-school setting. Religious leaders in the community may also be a resource. Remember, however, that they have commitments to their own faith. Be certain that any guest speaker understands the First Amendment guidelines for teaching about religion in public education and is clear about the academic nature of the assignment.

## 7. How Should I Treat Religious Holidays in the Classroom?

Teachers must be alert to the distinction between teaching about religious holidays, which is permissible, and celebrating religious holidays, which is not. Recognition of and information about holidays may focus on how and when they are celebrated, their origins, histories and generally agreed-upon meanings. If the approach is objective and sensitive, neither promoting nor inhibiting religion, this study can foster understanding and mutual respect for differences in belief. Teachers may not use the study of religious holidays as an opportunity to proselytize or otherwise inject personal religious beliefs into the discussion.

The use of religious symbols, provided they are used only as examples of cultural or religious heritage, is permissible as a teaching aid or resource. Religious symbols may be displayed only on a temporary basis as part of the academic lesson being studied. Students may choose to create artwork with religious symbols, but teachers should not assign or suggest such creations.

The use of art, drama, music or literature with religious themes is permissible if it serves a sound educational goal in the curriculum. Such themes should be included on the basis of their academic or aesthetic value, not as a vehicle for promoting religious belief. For example, sacred music may be sung or played as part of the academic study of music. School concerts that present a variety of selections may include religious music. Concerts should avoid programs dominated by religious music, especially when these coincide with a particular religious holiday.

This advice about religious holidays in public schools is based on consensus guidelines adopted by 18 educational and religious organizations.[4]

## 8. Are there Opportunities for Teacher Education in Study about Religion?

Teacher preparation and good academic resources are needed in order for study about religion in public schools to be constitutionally permissible and educationally sound.

The First Amendment Center supports initiatives in several regions of the country designed to prepare public-school teachers to teach about religion. The most extensive of these programs is the California 3Rs Project (Rights, Responsibilities, and Respect). Co-sponsored by the California County Superintendents Educational Services Association, the project has created a network of resource leaders and scholars throughout the state providing support for classroom teachers. Teachers trained by the project give workshops for their colleagues on the constitutional and educational guidelines for teaching about religion. Religious studies scholars from local colleges and universities are linked with school districts to provide ongoing expertise and periodic seminars on the religious traditions that teachers are discussing in the curriculum.

---

[4] "Religious Holidays and Public Schools: Questions and Answers" may be found in *Finding Common Ground*, available through the First Amendment Center.

The Utah State Office of Education co-sponsors a Utah 3Rs Project that is currently building a network of resource leaders in all of the state's school districts. Other states and districts have similar programs in various stages of development.[5]

Harvard University and the University of Pennsylvania offer master's level programs that are excellent opportunities for both current and prospective public- and private-school teachers interested in learning more about the study of religion and religious-liberty issues in American public life.[6]

Other colleges and universities offer assistance to teachers, including in-service programs focused on teaching about religion. A notable example is the Religion and Public Education Resource Center at California State University – Chico. This center provides resources, including curriculum guides and sample lessons in several subject areas.[7] Other organizations, such as the Council on Islamic Education, offer academic resources and workshops on teaching about specific religious traditions.[8]

### 9. What are Good Classroom Resources for Teaching about Religion?

Teaching about religion in the public schools requires that sound academic resources be made readily available to classroom teachers. Fortunately, good classroom resources, especially in the social studies, are now available for helping teachers integrate appropriate study about religion.

*Finding Common Ground: A First Amendment Guide to Religion and Public Education*, published by the First Amendment Center, provides an extensive list of organizations and publishers that offer classroom resources for teaching about religion in public schools.

Two recent publications are examples of what is now available for study about religion in a secondary school classroom:

---

[5] For details about "Rights, Responsibilities and Respect" programs, contact Marcia Beauchamp, Religious Freedom Programs Coordinator/First Amendment Center, Freedom Forum Pacific Coast Center, One Market St., Steuart Tower, 21st Floor, San Francisco, CA 94105, (415) 281-0900.

[6] For more information about the Program in Religion and Secondary Education at Harvard University, contact The Divinity School, 45 Francis Ave., Cambridge, MA 02138. Attention: Nancy Richardson, Director. Inquiries about the Religion in Public Life Certificate Program at the University of Pennsylvania should be addressed to Janet Theophano, Associate Director, Master of Liberal Arts Program, College of General Studies, University of Pennsylvania, 3440 Market St., Suite 100, Philadelphia, PA 19104-3335.

[7] Contact the Religion and Public Education Resource Center by writing to Dr. Bruce Grelle, Dept. of Religious Studies, California State University – Chico, Chico, CA 95929.

[8] The Council on Islamic Education may be reached by calling (714) 839-2929.

*Religion in American Life* is a 17-volume series written by leading scholars for young readers. Published by Oxford University Press, the series includes three chronological volumes on the religious history of the U.S., nine volumes covering significant religious groups (Protestants, Catholics, Jews, Orthodox Christians, Mormons, Muslims, Hindus, Buddhists, Native Americans and others), and four volumes addressing specific topics of special importance for understanding the role of religion in American life (women and religion, church-state issues, African American religion, and immigration).[9]

Columbia University Press has published a CD-ROM entitled *On Common Ground: World Religions in America.* This multimedia resource uses text, primary sources, photographs, music, film, and the spoken word to bring alive the extraordinary religious diversity in the United States. Fifteen different religions in various regions of America are represented, from the long-established Christian, Jewish, and Native American traditions to the more recent arrivals such as Hinduism and Buddhism.[10]

## 10. What is the Relationship between Religion and Character Education?

As discussed above, the First Amendment prohibits public-school teachers from either inculcating or inhibiting religion. Teachers must remain neutral concerning religion, neutral among religions and neutral between religion and non-religion. But this does not mean that teachers should be neutral concerning civic virtue or moral character.

Teachers should teach the personal and civic virtues widely held in our society, such as honesty, caring, fairness, and integrity. They must do so without either invoking religious authority or denigrating the religious or philosophical commitments of students and parents.

When school districts develop a plan for comprehensive character education, they should keep in mind that the moral life of a great many Americans is shaped by deep religious conviction. Both the approach to character education and the classroom materials used should be selected in close consultation with parents and other community members representing a broad range of perspectives. When care is taken to find consensus, communities are able to agree on the core character traits they wish taught in the schools and how they wish character education to be done.

---

[9] For more information about the Oxford University Press series, *Religion in American Life*, call (800) 451-7556.

[10] For more information about the CD-ROM *On Common Ground: World Religions in America*, call (800) 944-8648.

For guidance on how to develop and implement a quality character education program, contact the Character Education Partnership in Washington, D.C.[11]

## The Personal Beliefs of Teachers

### 11. May I Pray or Otherwise Practice My Faith While at School?

As employees of the government, public-school teachers are subject to the Establishment Clause of the First Amendment and thus required to be neutral concerning religion while carrying out their duties as teachers. That means, for example, that teachers do not have the right to pray with or in the presence of students during the school day.

Outside of their school responsibilities, public-school teachers are free like other citizens to teach or otherwise participate in their local religious community. But teachers must refrain from using their position in the public school to promote their outside religious activities.

Teachers, of course, bring their faith with them through the schoolhouse door each morning. Because of the First Amendment, however, teachers who wish to pray or engage in other religious activities—unless they are silent— should do so outside the presence of students. If a group of teachers wishes to meet for prayer or scriptural study in the faculty lounge during their free time in the school day, we see no constitutional reason why they may not be permitted to do so as long as the activity is outside the presence of students and does not interfere with their duties or the rights of other teachers.

Teachers are permitted to wear non-obtrusive jewelry, such as a cross or Star of David. But teachers should not wear clothing with a proselytizing message (e.g., a "Jesus Saves" T-shirt).

### 12. How do I Respond if Students Ask about My Religious Beliefs?

Some teachers prefer not to answer the question, stating that it is inappropriate for a teacher to inject personal beliefs into the discussion. Other teachers may choose to answer the question straightforwardly and succinctly in the interest of an open and honest classroom environment.

Before answering the question, however, teachers should consider the age of the students. Middle and high school students may be able to distinguish between a personal view and the official position of the school; very young children may not. In any case, the teacher may answer at most with a brief statement of personal belief—but may not turn the question into an

---

[11] The Character Education Partnership is located at 918 16th St., NW, Suite 501, Washington, DC 20006. Call (800) 988-8081. Web site: www.character.org

opportunity to proselytize for or against religion. Teachers may neither reward nor punish students because they agree or disagree with the religious views of the teacher.

## Religious Expression of Students

### 13. May Students Express Religious Views in Public Schools?

In "Religion in the Public Schools: A Joint Statement of Current Law," 35 religious and civil liberties organizations give the following summary of the rights of students to express their faith in a public school:

> Students have the right to pray individually or in groups or to discuss their religious views with their peers so long as they are not disruptive. Because the Establishment Clause does not apply to purely private speech, students enjoy the right to read their Bibles or other scriptures, say grace before meals, pray before tests, and discuss religion with other willing student listeners. In the classroom, students have the right to pray quietly except when required to be actively engaged in school activities (e.g., students may not decide to pray just as a teacher calls on them). In informal settings, such as the cafeteria or in the halls, students may pray either audibly or silently, subject to the same rules of order as apply to other speech in these locations. However, the right to engage in voluntary prayer does not include, for example, the right to have a captive audience listen or to compel other students to participate.[12]

### 14. May Students Express Religious Views in Their Assignments?

"Religious Expression in Public Schools," guidelines published by the U.S. Department of Education, offers the following guidance about religious expression in student assignments:

> Students may express their beliefs about religion in the form of homework, artwork, and other written and oral assignments free of discrimination based on the religious content of their submissions. Such home and classroom work should be judged by ordinary academic standards of substance and relevance, and against other legitimate pedagogical concerns identified by the school.[13]

---

[12] "Religion in the Public Schools: A Joint Statement of Current Law" may be obtained by writing: "Religion in the Public Schools," 15 East 84th St., Suite 501, New York, NY 10028.
[13] Copies of the U.S. Department of Education guidelines may be obtained by calling 1-800-USA-LEARN.

## 15. How Should Public Schools Respond to Excusal Requests from Parents?

In "A Parent's Guide to Religion in the Public Schools," the National PTA and the First Amendment Center give the following advice concerning excusal requests:

> Whenever possible, school officials should try to accommodate the requests of parents and students for excusal from classroom discussions or activities for religious reasons. If focused on a specific discussion, assignment, or activity, such requests should be routinely granted in order to strike a balance between the student's religious freedom and the school's interest in providing a well-rounded education. If it is proved that particular lessons substantially burden a student's free exercise of religion and if the school cannot prove a compelling interest in requiring attendance, some courts may require the school to excuse the students.[14]

## 16. May Public Schools Accommodate Students with Special Religious Needs?

Public schools are sometimes asked to accommodate students with special religious needs or practices. Sensitive and thoughtful school officials may easily grant many of these requests without raising constitutional questions. Muslim students, for example, may need a quiet place at lunch or during breaks to fulfill their prayer obligation during the school day. Jehovah's Witnesses ask for their children to be excused from birthday celebrations. As long as honoring these requests is feasible, school officials should do so in the spirit of the First Amendment.

Administrators and teachers should not, however, be placed in the position of monitoring a child's compliance with a particular religious requirement. Enforcing religious obligations such as prayer, dietary restrictions, or wearing a head covering is the responsibility of parents, not teachers.[15]

## 17. May Students form Extracurricular Religious Clubs?

The Equal Access Act passed by Congress in 1984 ensures that students in secondary public schools may form religious clubs, including Bible clubs, if the school allows other "noncurriculum-related groups." The Act is intended to protect student-initiated and student-led meetings in secondary schools.

---

[14] Copies of "A Parent's Guide to Religion and the Public Schools," published by the National PTA and the First Amendment Center, are available free from the First Amendment Center.

[15] A good resource for understanding the religious needs and practices of students is *America's Religions: An Educator's Guide to Beliefs and Practices* by Benjamin J. Hubbard, John T. Hatfield, and James A. Santucci. It is available from Teacher Ideas Press by calling (800) 237-6124.

According to the Act, outsiders may not "direct, conduct, control, or regularly attend" student religious clubs, and teachers acting as monitors may be present at religious meetings in a nonparticipatory capacity only.[16]

The U.S. Department of Education in "Religious Expression in Public Schools" gives the following guidance for interpreting the Equal Access Act:

> The Equal Access Act is designed to ensure that, consistent with the First Amendment, student religious activities are accorded the same access to public school facilities as are student secular activities. Based on decisions of the Federal courts, as well as its interpretations of the Act, the Department of Justice has advised that the Act should be interpreted as providing, among other things, that:
>
> · Student religious groups at public secondary schools have the same right of access to school facilities as is enjoyed by other comparable student groups. Under the Equal Access Act, a school receiving Federal funds that allows one or more student noncurriculum-related clubs to meet on its premises during noninstructional time may not refuse access to student religious groups.
>
> · A meeting, as defined and protected by the Equal Access Act, may include a prayer service, Bible reading, or other worship exercise.
>
> · A school receiving Federal funds must allow student groups meeting under the Act to use the school media—including the public address system, the school newspaper, and the school bulletin board—to announce their meetings on the same terms as other noncurriculum-related student groups are allowed to use the school media. Any policy concerning the use of school media must be applied to all noncurriculum-related student groups in a nondiscriminatory manner. Schools, however, may inform students that certain groups are not school-sponsored.
>
> · A school creates a limited open forum under the Equal Access Act, triggering equal access rights for religious groups, when it allows students to meet during their lunch periods or other noninstructional time during the school day, as well as when it allows students to meet before and after the school day.

## 18. May Students Distribute Religious Literature in School?

An increasing number of students are requesting permission to distribute religious literature on public-school campuses. According to the guidelines issued by the U.S. Department of Education:

---

[16] The requirements of the Equal Access Act are described in detail in "Equal Access and the Public Schools: Questions and Answers," a pamphlet sponsored by 21 religious and educational groups. The full text is contained in *Finding Common Ground*, available through the First Amendment Center.

Students have a right to distribute religious literature to their schoolmates on the same terms as they are permitted to distribute other literature that is unrelated to school curriculum or activities. Schools may impose the same reasonable time, place, and manner or other constitutional restrictions on distribution of religious literature as they do on nonschool literature generally, but they may not single out religious literature for special regulation.

This statement is reprinted with the permission of:
First Amendment Center
1207 18th Avenue South
Nashville, TN 37212
(615) 321-9588
www.freedomforum.org

For additional copies, call
1-800-830-3733 and request Publication No. 99-F02.

# BIBLIOGRAPHY

Adler, Mortimer J. (1982). *The Paideia Proposal: An Educational Manifesto*. New York: Macmillan.

Anderson, Ronald D. (1996). *Study of Curriculum Reform*. Washington, DC: U.S. Government Printing Office.

Behe, Michael. (1996). *Darwin's Black Box: The Biochemical Challenge to Evolution*. New York: Free Press.

Benson, B. E. (2002). "What It Means to Be Secular: A Conversation with Philosopher Charles Taylor," *Books and Culture*, July/August 2002, p. 37.

Borg, Marcus J. and Wright, N. T. (1999). *The Meaning of Jesus: Two Visions*. San Francisco: HarperSanFrancisco.

Carter, Stephen L. (1993). *The Culture of Disbelief*. New York: Basic Books.

Cheney, Lynne V. (1987). *American Memory: A Report on the Humanities in the Nation's Public Schools*. Washington, DC: National Endowment for the Humanities.

Clapp, Rodney (2000). *Border Crossings*. Grand Rapids, MI: Brazos Press.

Cobern, William W. (1991). *World View Theory and Science Education Research*. Manhattan, KS: National Association for Research in Science Teaching.

Dembski, William A. (1999). *Intelligent Design: The Bridge between Science and Theology*. Downers Grove, IL: InterVarsity Press.

Easterbrook, Gregg (1997). "Science and God: A Warming Trend?" *Science*, vol. 277, pp. 890 – 93, August 15, 1997.

Eisner, Elliot W. (1992). "Curriculum Ideologies," in Jackson, Philip W., ed. *Handbook of Research on Curriculum*. New York: Macmillan. pp. 302 – 26.

Fowler, James W. (1981). *Stages of Faith: The Psychology of Human Development and the Quest for Meaning*. New York: HarperSanFrancisco.

Fraser, James W. (1999). *Between Church and State: Religion & Public Education in a Multicultural America*. New York: St. Martin's Griffin.

Fullan, Michael (2001). *The New Meaning of Educational Change,* 3 ed. New York: Teachers College Press.

Gallagher, Susan V. and Lundin, Roger (1989). *Literature through the Eyes of Faith*. New York: Harper & Row.

Gardner, Howard (1999). *The Disciplined Mind: What All Students Should Understand*. New York: Simon & Schuster.

Gardner, Howard (1983). *Frames of Mind: The Theory of Multiple Intelligences*. New York: Basic Books.

Gardner, Howard (1999). Who Owns Intelligence? *The Atlantic Monthly*. February, p. 71.

Giberson, Karl W. (2002). (An interview of Paul Davies). "God and Time Machines," *Books and Culture*, March/April, p. 29.

Goodlad, John I. (1994). *What Schools Are For*, 2 ed. Bloomington, IN: Phi Delta Kappa Educational Foundation.

Goodlad, John I. (1994). What Schools Are For, 2 ed. Bloomington, IN: Phi Delta Kappa Educational Foundation, pp. 46-52. As quoted in Goodlad, John I. and Timothy J. McMannon, eds. (1997). *The Public Purpose of Education and Schooling*. San Francisco: Jossey-Bass.

Grenz, Stanley J. (1996). *A Primer on Postmodernism*. Grand Rapids, MI: Eerdmans.

Griffin, Greg (2002). "Ethics Debate Muscles Way into Business Schools," *Denver Post*, July 28, 2002, p. 1K.

Himmelfarb, Gertrude (1999). *One Nation, Two Cultures*. New York: Alfred A. Knopf.

Hirsch, E. D., Jr. (1987). *Cultural Literacy: What Every American Needs to Know*. Boston: Houghton Mifflin.

Hunter, James Davison (2000). *The Death of Character: Moral Education in an Age without Good or Evil*. New York: Basic Books.

Johnson, Philip E. (1997). *Defeating Darwinism by Opening Minds*. Downers Grove, IL: InterVarsity Press.

Kessler, Rachael (2000). *The Soul of Education*. Alexandria, VA: Association for Supervision and Curriculum Development.

Levinson, David (1996). *Religion: A Cross-Cultural Encyclopedia*. New York: Oxford University Press.

Marty, Martin E. (2000). *Education, Religion, and the Common Good*. San Francisco: Jossey-Bass.

McGrath, Alister E. (1999). *Christian Spirituality*. Oxford: Blackwell Publishers.

McMannon, Timothy J. "The Changing Purposes of Education and Schooling," in Goodlad, John I. and Timothy J. McMannon, eds. (1997). *The Public Purpose of Education and Schooling*. San Francisco: Jossey-Bass.

Nash, Robert J. (1999). *Faith, Hype and Clarity: Teaching about Religion in American Schools and Colleges*. New York: Teachers College Press.

National Commission on Excellence in Education (1983). *A Nation at Risk.* Washington, DC: U.S. Government Printing Office.

National Council of Teachers of Mathematics (1989). *Curriculum and Evaluation Standards for School Mathematics.* Reston, VA: NCTM.

National Research Council (1996). *National Science Education Standards.* Washington, DC: National Academy Press.

National Research Council (1998). *Teaching about Evolution and the Nature of Science.* Washington, DC: National Academy Press.

Noddings, Nel (1993). *Educating for Intelligent Belief and Unbelief.* New York: Teachers College Press.

Nord, Warren A. (1995). *Religion and American Education: Rethinking a National Dilemma.* Chapel Hill, NC: University of North Carolina Press.

Nord, Warren A. and Haynes, Charles C. (1998). *Taking Religion Seriously across the Curriculum.* Alexandria, VA: Association for Supervision and Curriculum Development.

Pinar, William F. and Grumet, M. R. (1976). *Toward a Poor Curriculum.* Dubuque, IA: Kendall/Hunt.

Polkinghorne, John and Welker, Michael (2001). *Faith in the Living God.* Minneapolis: Fortress Press.

Probst, Robert E. (1991). "Response to Literature," in Flood, James, et al., eds. *Handbook of Research on Teaching the English Language Arts.* New York: Macmillan.

Purves, Alan C. (1991). "The School Subject Literature," in Flood, James, et al., eds. *Handbook of Research on Teaching the English Language Arts.* New York: Macmillan.

Raymo, Chet. (1998). *Skeptics and True Believers.* New York: Walker and Company.

Riley, Richard W. (1998). *Religious Expression in Public Schools.* Washington, DC: U.S. Department of Education.

Sarason, Seymour. (1990). *The Predictable Failure of Educational Reform.* San Francisco: Jossey-Bass.

Schubert, William H. (1986). *Curriculum: Perspective, Paradigm, and Possibility.* New York: Macmillan.

Scott, Eugenie C. *The Creation/Evolution Continuum.* www.ncseweb.org.

Sears, James T. and Carper, James C. (1998). *Curriculum, Religion and Public Education.* New York: Teachers College Press.

Sire, James W. (1997). *The Universe Next Door: A Basic Worldview Catalog,* 3 ed. Downers Grove, IL: InterVarsity Press.

Sizer, T. R. and Sizer, N. F. (1999). *The Students Are Watching.* Boston: Beacon Press.

Smith, Huston (2001). *Why Religion Matters.* New York: HarperSanFrancisco.

Tyack, David B. and Cuban, Larry. (1995). *Tinkering toward Utopia.* Cambridge, MA: Harvard University Press.

# INDEX

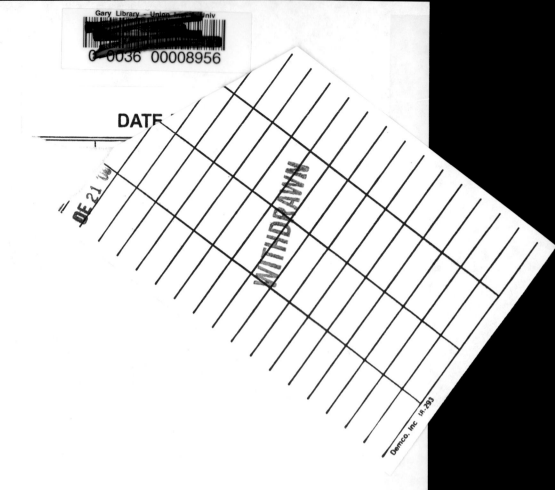